The GRIMPEBBET ALMANAC

James Howerton

iUniverse, Inc.
Bloomington

THE GRIMPEBBET ALMANAC

iUniverse books may be ordered through booksellers or by contacting:

iUniverse
1663 Liberty Drive
Bloomington, IN 47403
www.iuniverse.com
1-800-Authors (1-800-288-4677)

ISBN: 978-1-4697-3853-6 (sc)
ISBN: 978-1-4697-3854-3 (ebk)

Printed in the United States of America

iUniverse rev. date: 02/17/2012

The Grimpebbet Almanac

Issue # One

News and political quotes
Recipes and farm information
Tasteful cartoons
Historical facts and figures
Decent advertisements

J.D. Baghead, Editor in Chief

(The price of this almanac is five dollars. If you send us five dollars, we will wish you an enjoyable and educational journey through the following magical pages. If not, and you read further than this page, or peek at the cartoons, you are in violation of Federal Law. You have been informed that Federal law protects the lawful rights of this publication. And God forgive you—no, God damn you if you read any further than this without sending us five dollars. That's five dollars per copy, so your friends have to pay for it too. Put it down and shudder in disgust right now if you don't plan to pay for it. Or pay us five dollars per copy for it, and be transported into a world of magic that is worth a lot more than five bucks. One thing or another, just don't Steal it. Don't go beyond this page without paying us five bucks, each and every one of you. We don't mind being shunned and hated, just don't rip us off. We're informing you, as any responsible business would do, that the price of this almanac is five dollars. Don't turn the page if you haven't sent us five bucks. No, don't do it. Don't even think about doing it if you haven't sent us the money. Don't do it . . .)

"Only by breeding loyalty to royalty can
you ensure a monarchy that is sound, wise
and noble."
—King George the Third

A Corporate moment:

"Sir, I'm sorry to say that this new drug does not cure cancer."
"What? Viagra doesn't—all the millions—"
"I'm sorry, Sir, but I'm afraid all it does is give the male rats enormous errections."
"All the money spent on this drug—and you're telling me that all it does is........!"

Near Death Experiences you never hear about.

"Wow, you're Napoleon? I had no idea you were so short!"
—the first casualty of the war

"Hey, we don't serve lawyers here!"

Order now, from the Grimpebbet Almanac's Collector Series, the most collectible Bobble-Head dolls ever:

Rush Limbaugh
Michael Moore
Sean Hannity
Al Franken
Cal Thomas
Nancy Pelosi

Bop them on the head and watch them nod! Hours of entertainment! Order them now, before these bobble-head dolls lose importance and collection value. Ask them the most hypocritical questions and then Bop them on the head. We guarantee you they will nod Every time. A riot at parties!

(Visa and Mastercards grudgingly accepted, also checks, but we do prefer cash)

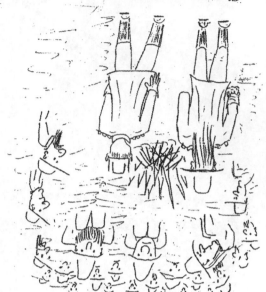

Gettysburg, that has a peaceful
Sound to it. We'll let the men
Rest up here.

I named my boy Pissonya.
That way I knew he'd grow up
tough.

From the Unpublished Journal of Buffalo Bill Cody:
"The rarest sight on the Great Plains is the White Buffalo. Lucky is the man who can cast his eyes on such a sight, for he has seen the greatest wonder of all. If he can kill the beast he is luckier still, as the White is the tastiest of all the buffalo."

Even the fearsome Ghengis Khan had a playful side.

```
SISSYS MAY SHARE COMMON GENETIC LINK, SCIENTISTS SAY
   (New gene--punkass 9--discovered by MIT researchers)
```

The Kelsey brothers just loved watching 3 Stooges movies.

AMERICANS ARE RUDE, foreign diplomat charges: "They laughed at me and made me feel uncomfortable," claims Dr. Mohammed Fatass.

RIOT BREAKS OUT AT BROWN PAPER BAGS CONCERT! SEVERAL INJURED!

Rival gangs are to blame, claims combo spokesperson. The Star City Skeletons, a Lincoln Biker gang, notorious for boodlerism and improper behavior, held up placards proclaiming, "BROWN PAPER BAGS SUCK!". Another gang, the Rural Devil Worshippers And Cattle Mutilators, held up a contrary sign saying, "BROWN PAPER BAGS REALLY SUCK!". Star City Skeletons leader Pug Odonowitz ignited the riot by crying out, "Brown Paper Bags suck, but they don't Really suck!".

Words were exchanged concerning whether the controversial trio sucked or Really sucked, until violence errupted, and mayhem exploded at the famed M & N's Sandwich Shoppe. Brown Paper Bags, instigators of the riot, were reported by onlookers to be "cowering and smirking in the corner, content with the mischief they had created." Lancaster County Police gave the odious combo 24 hours to leave the city of Lincoln.

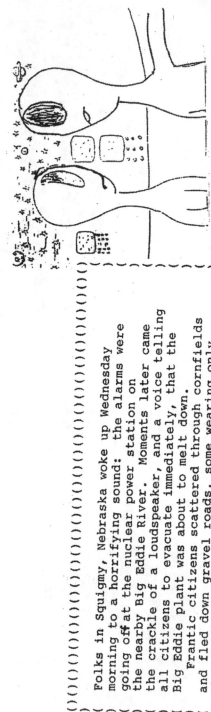

"It's the Earth Delegation. They're looking for something called—a bathroom?"

"You're off the Chess Team, Fulton. Seems you tested positive for steroids."

Folks in Squigmy, Nebraska woke up Wednesday morning to a horrifying sound: the alarms were going off at the nuclear power station on the nearby Big Eddie River. Moments later came the crackle of a loudspeaker, and a voice telling all citizens to evacuate immediately, that the Big Eddie plant was about to melt down.
Frantic citizens scattered through cornfields and fled down gravel roads, some wearing only their sleepwear. Over four hours went by before order was restored and incident found to be a hoax.
"I always wanted to play a real hooter of a joke," said Earl Steinbottom, former plant manager.

Are you a liar and a cheat? We don't think so, we think you're a pretty honest Joe—or Joe-ess. That's why we're asking you to fill out our own political survey! Come on, it'll be fun, and you'll be fulfilling your patriotic duty. It will tell us if you are a good decent patriotic American, or a tapeworm living in and eating out the guts of our great nation.

Okay, no cheating, please.

OUR OWN POLITICAL SURVEY:

1. If you criticize the current administration, should you be shot:

    A) Without a trial, under the Terrorist Act?
    B) After a fair trial?

2. Most of the candidates running for president have stopped using illegal drugs.

    TRUE   or   FALSE   (please circle your answer)

3. A JFK haircut on a Democratic candidate is purely coincidental.

    TRUE   or   FALSE

4. The American economy performs better when we have a president who gets pussy on the side.

    TRUE   or   FALSE

5. Will you vote Democrat, even though they are a hollow mockery of a party full of poopy wimps who live in La-La Land—or will you vote Republican and risk bankruptcy, corporate slavery and—well, maybe concentration camps?

    REP   or   DEM

6. It's not called COW NEWS, you clueless liberal whiny-baby. It's called FOX NEWS. Are you too stoned to get it?

    YES   or   NO

7. Essay Question (50 words or less, please): Is it possible for Right Wing Conservatives to have fun, and why not?

8. Bill O'Reilly and Al Franken finally shut their pie holes and get it on in the parking lot. Which answer indicates the most likely outcome:

   A) O'Reilly, tall and strapping, slaps Franken's glasses off his face, and Franken collapses into a fetal pile of liberal Wah!—and begins to weep.
   B) Franken's high school wrestling instincts suddenly take over, his compassion vanishes, and he brutally goes on the attack, rolling the smirking, Heydrich-looking Right Wing Monster into a human pretzel.
   C) O'Reilly's Irish blood boils, and he goes after the Jew much as his forefathers did, mindlessly clubbing away with ham-shaped fists.
   D) Franken outwits the furious Mick, sidesteps and puts on a move that requires O'Reilly to cry for his mother.
   E) All of the above.

A DISCLAIMER

Now that you've sampled the Grimpebbet Almanac, you should realize that we need a pretty hefty disclaimer to avoid getting sued. This is it, and we're sure that it will stand up in court, because it's true.

NO FAMOUS PERSON, HISTORICAL OR OTHERWISE is quoted in this almanac. No well know personality is quoted. At all. Other people have the same name as you, you famous arrogant bastards. Just because you're famous doesn't mean when somebody writes your name he's referring to you. The universe doesn't revolve around famous, arrogant overpaid jerks like you.

If we say, for example, that Joseph Smith was insane, we're referring not to any historical figure, but to old Joe Smith, the nutty guy who goes through the trash cans. You get it? Don't even think about suing us, we'll eat your lunch. Quotes attributed to famous people are all purely coincidental.

There's a guy who lives down the street, goes by the name Buffalo Bill. Don't we have the right to quote this guy without the other Buffalo Bill suing our asses? Let me give you another example: Abraham Lincoln, was a heavy pot smoker. You gasp and you groan until you learn that we went to high school with a guy who's name was-we kid you not-Abe Lincoln. And he was a heavy pot smoker.

So the other Abe Lincoln decides to sue us? Bring it on, string bean. Your name doesn't give you the right to sue anybody. That goes to any famous person out there we might coincidentally embarrass. You can't sue us, because there are folks out there with the same name as you, and it's these folks we're quoting, not you.

So ha ha ha, you pusses. Try to sue us and we'll hire Mark Geragos and he'll put you in the Puss Hall of Fame. Don't clench your butt cheeks if your name appears in this almanac. Relax, we're not talking about you. Yes, we know, you're famous, you're sensitive, we feel your pain. Oh, boo hoo, Wah!

But, you see, we're not talking about you. We want to make that clear to the judge before any trial gets started. If a friend of ours is quoted in this almanac and he or she happens to have the same name as some famous twit, it's purely coincidental.

One more thing, famous person who's thinking about suing us: we have friends too, friends with baseball bats. And they're not as refined as your friends.

You sabby that?

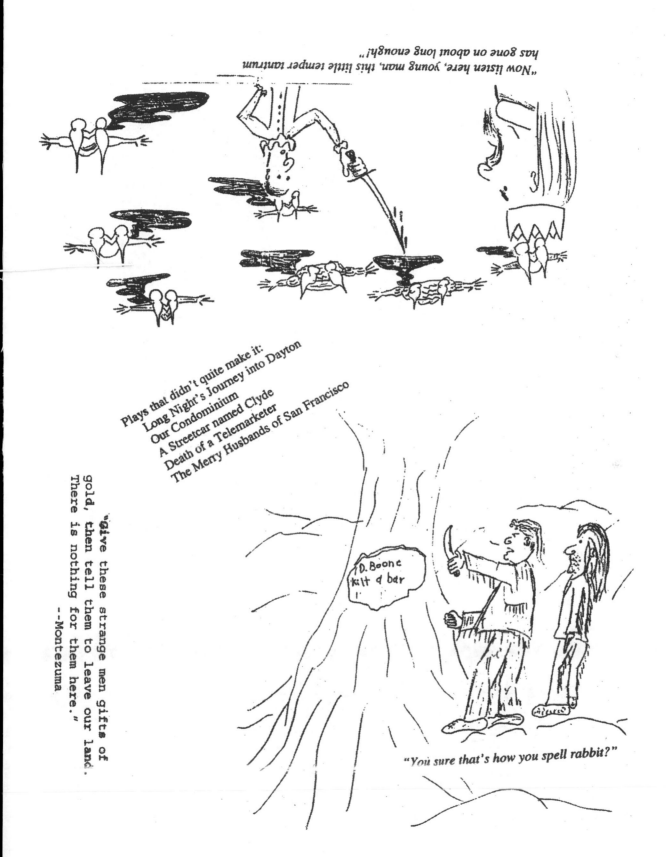

"Now listen here, young man, this little temper tantrum has gone on about long enough!"

Plays that didn't quite make it:
Long Night's Journey into Dayton
Our Condominium
A Streetcar named Clyde
Death of a Telemarketer
The Merry Husbands of San Francisco

"Give these strange men gifts of
gold, then tell them to leave our land.
There is nothing for them here."
--Montezuma.

"You sure that's how you spell rabbit?"

9

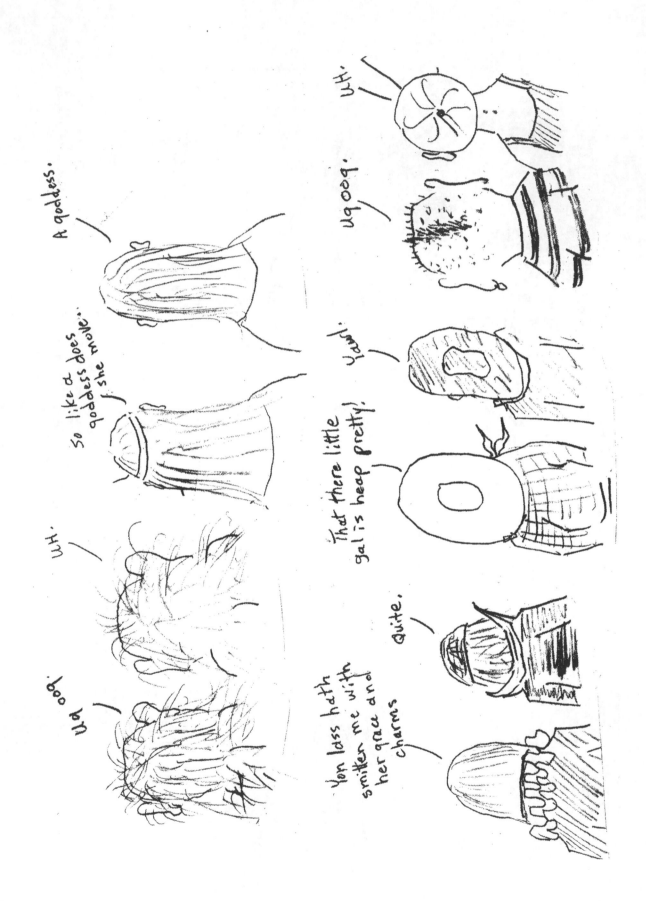

10

TALES OF THE PIONEERS . . . by Wilma Bumpers

You kids have got it pretty easy these days, if you ask me. But life wasn't so easy for the pioneers. When I was a little girl we had no indoor plumbing. That meant when you had to take a shit, you went out back to the outhouse and you wiped with the Sears Catalog. There wasn't anything remarkable about going to the toilet in the those days, except when the wind chill reached 60 below. But the prairie had shaped and toughened us, and we had great endurance and sturdy bowels.

Of course we all yearned for an indoor toilet, but Father forbade it. He had seen one in the city and he called it "The Devil's Machine". He was an old world man with old world values. So it was a great relief to us all when he died, and Mother celebrated by purchasing the most expensive toilet in the Sears Catalog. It was a porcelain and chrome beauty, and we named her Molly.

This new addition to our prairie family created many amusing anecdotes, such as the first time Grandma Bumpers heard it flush and thought an earthquake was occurring and fell dead of a heart attack. Or the time our cousins from the city came to visit and went swimming in the pond out back and we did not tell them that it was the sewer pond.

Yes, fond are the memories of Molly, who stood at her post for many years. And I am not ashamed to admit that I cried on the day big Uncle Amos broke poor Molly for good.

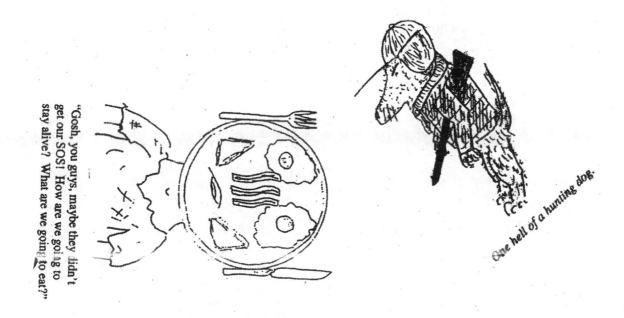

"Gosh, you guys, maybe they didn't get our SOS! How are we going to stay alive? What are we going to eat?"

One hell of a hunting dog.

11

EARN BIG MONEY WITH A DEGREE IN SUPERNATURAL STUDIES!

Do you have a desperate need to believe anything as long as it's not true? Why not put that valuable skill to use in the growing field of Supernaturalism? One of the fastest growing industries in America, Supernaturalism (don't let the technical terms scare you), is an ancient and proven science that is being practiced by millions. Its basic tenet is that if a phenomenon cannot be proven to be false, then it must be true. And it can never be proven to be anything if I say it can't. See how easy it is?

How can you make money off this new and exciting field of study? Well, with a degree from the Institute of Supernatural Studies, you can obtain the skills you need to make people believe anything. Imagine your own talk show, or a line of books and videotapes. Imagine gathering hundreds of stupefied followers into your religious cult! Imagine your own sofa on the Psychic Hotline Show! Appearances on talk shows and all the other reknown forums of thought and culture! Millions will idolize you after you put your new skills to use! Act now:

Spring 1998 classes available by mail:
*ELFOLOGY. Learn the secrets to tracking down and capturing the little men of the forest.
*THIS BUSINESS OF WATER WITCHING
*CRYSTALS, PYRAMIDS, MAGIC ROCKS AND CHANTING 101
*ENTRAIL READING. Learn how to tell the future by reading the large intestines of goats.
*SPRING BIOLOGY FIELD TRIP. Study the Loch Ness Monster in its native environment.
*ALIEN ENCOUNTERS
*GHOSTOLOGY
*THE STUDY OF QUANTUM ASTROLOGY
*PARAPSYCHOLOGY. Learn how to psychoanalyze spirits of the dead, poltergeists, banshees and hobgoblins
*PSYCHOLOGY. Learn how to analyze terra-based hominid organisms
*PSYCHIC RHETORIC. Learn the skills necessary to counter facts and logic
*ESP.
*GOVERNMENT CONSPIRACIES.
*PRE-WITCHCRAFT. Includes lab
*PRE-WIZARDRY. Includes lab

"Ms. Hansen, kindergarten can be a fun
and happy experience for little Patrick,
or it can be rough. That's entirely up to you."

"WE ARE THE HOLLOW MEN"

A bank clerk named Tom Eliot wrote those words many years ago. He was talking about financial insecurity.

Is your retirement fund going to leave you sitting in a dank corner eating adult baby food? Can you look into the eyes of the next generation and be sure they'll care for you when you're old and helpless? Social Security? Ha. Fact is, if you haven't picked up yet that money is pretty darned important—right up there with Peace and Love and Woodstock—then you're likely to wind up financially "hollow".

Don't let that happen. Call AMERICAN POETS FINANCIAL SERVICES right now!

"It is a lie that I fiddled
while Rome burned. I put on
my sister's clothing and danced
while Rome burned."
--Nero

"We can't conceive of zero, of nothing. That is because by definition it cannot exist. Nothing is impossible to achieve, because it will reach a point at which nothing itself becomes something."

--Babe Ruth

News Quotes of the Day:

James Carville: "It's like that ole hound down there in the swamp used to say, you can skin a possum, but can you provide it with universal health coverage?"

Mary Matalin: "My God, I'm having sex with that guy!"

Laura Ingram: "How many left-wing liberal guys are out there watching me, listening to me, thinking 'I can tame you, Baby, I can tame you!'—spanking me until I scream out, 'JFK! Oh, God—Oh, yeah! JFK! JFK!'"

Sean Hannity: "I submit to you-the Real American Heroes among us-I submit to you that I am more patriotic than Michael Savage (his real name, by the way, is Michael Weiner). I know that might cause you to gasp, or whatever-okay! I have the courage, and I'm not ashamed to admit that I, Sean Hannity, am more of a Real Patriotic American than Michael Savage. Now, let me say, Michael Weiner-I mean Savage—is a friend of mine, a good friend. But his style . . . ."

Michael Wei-Savage: "You know, members of the Savage Nation-you know-Sean Hannity is a good great friend of mine. I love Sean, he's a great commentator and a pretty good American. But every now and then he gets-what's the word-Seduced, that's it-he gets Seduced into thinking that maybe those raghead Islamies aren't so vile and evil after all. See, I know you'll understand because you're listening to this show, and you wouldn't be if you weren't smarter than everybody else and able to see the truth. And the truth is that Sean sometimes buys into the liberal left wing-garbage they're spewing in our faces. Sean's against the idea of putting a fence up between us and Mexico. Like it's okay to let a billion or so bean-eating Mexicans come into our country and take our jobs. You might believe that, Sean, but I have to agree with the Bible when it says, 'Good Fences Make Good neighbors' . . . ."

Al Franken: "How strange. Now that I'm no longer funny, people are making me into a celebrity . . . ."

Walter Cronkite: "One thing sailing has taught me. You finally get too old to give a rat's ass . . . ."

"A what? A Whiskey Rebellion? Jesus Christ, this country isn't going to last a year."

--George Washington

Attendance was low at opening of new Musical, "Those Lovable Germans".

The Human Torch realizes that he must forever remain celibate.

DRUG ADDICTION HAS NO EFFECT ON SELF ESTEEM, Harvard professor claims. Cites Rush Limbaugh as proof.

THE LAST WORD.....

by Pastor Milton Crane

"The man burst into my church and interrupted my sermon. He had long ragged hair and a beard, and he was dressed like one of those street people, in a filthy moth-eaten robe and sandals. I saw at once that he was insane, and that there was going to be trouble.

"My fears were realized when all at once the madman began grabbing up the collection plates and throwing them and their monetary contents onto the floor. He was ranting something about defiling the temple of God with money and splendor. The entire congregation was horrified. I immediately called the authorities and had him arrested."

INTERMISSION . . . . with Cornfield Johnny

This page is what the Grimpebbet Almanac folks like to call "The Intermission".

We've all worked hard to bring you a serious and comprehensive over-view of important events, weather forecasts and farm information. In addition to these community services, we'd like to think we've also entertained you. That's why our staff of writers strives to their ass cheeks to bring you- our beloved reader-the best of American fiction and literary entertainment.

Have we neglected sports? No, no, no we have not. Have we neglected the recipes? I think not, as you'll find several tasty masterpieces in this tome. Have we made a difference?

Well, that's what it's all about, isn't it? Have we, the Grimpebbet Almanac, touched your lives and lifted your spirits?

Shit, as far as that goes, you can get your spirits lifted in any of those other fancy almanacs with their glossy paper and pictures of naked women- go on ahead!

But when that big city horse manure (please excuse the language), leaves you wondering . . . . maybe . . . . just maybe . . . . I might want something more out of my almanac. I might want serious reading for those who think! We hope you'll keep us in mind, that you'll dump them and come aboard with us.

If you've liked our work so far, please don't hesitate to send us money so that we can continue this fine tradition.

—you know what, it's Intermission time. So let's all get up, stretch, take a deep breath, scratch what needs to be scratched, and go on to PART TWO.

A MESSAGE FROM THE GRIMPEBBET ALMANAC—(send us money now and you may qualify to join our Special Friends Club! Don't be stupid about this, send us money now, today, before it's too late and you miss out!)

They rose form a stinky recording studio in an abandoned chicken house to become the cutting-edge satire trio of the century! They blew other comedy acts like Weird Al and Cher completely off the map!

Brown Paper Bags are so weird and wacky and irrelevant-irreverent-that once you listen to them you will piss your pants-then you'll shit your pants! Then you'll barf up your breakfast!

We promise, if these songs on this CD aren't incontinently funny, then you let us know about it, will you?

You have our guarantee-if there isn't a mess of shit and piss on your floor after you listen to this CD, and if you're not on the floor choking on your own vomit-then we're not as funny as we think we are. But we are. You'd be a fuckhead to even doubt it.

Do you dare listen to Brown Paper Bags? Do you, you pussy? Come on, Puss, have you got the guts? Let's see if you got the guts—you Puss-to actually pay for this music and then listen to it. Come on, puss-puss-Pussy. We dare you.

Buy our CD, Pussy—if you dare.

LETTERS TO THE EDITOR:

Dear Baghead: Don't even think of putting out another one of these putrid piles of rubbish. The contents of this newsletter stank so badly that I had to ask my wife to dispose of it for me. Your writing is below comment, and your ideas of less value than worm boogars. I am ashamed that you call yourself a Nebraskan. You and those misfits and butt-brains the Brown Paper Bags should be tossed, like refuse, from the top of the state capital building.
Sincerely,

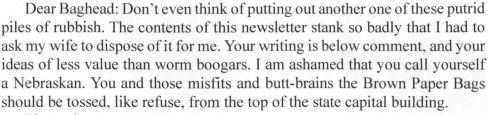

Dr. A. Richards (Pimwell, NE)

Deer Baghead,

You rool, man! Me and my collige buddies read
The GA all the time! It's the best for good riting and
Informashun. Keep up the good work.
B. Kosmiki (UNL Seenyor)

Dear Punk: I have your address now, smart boy. You put your address in this newsletter, and now I have it, and you know what that means. I'll be coming over to see you. Do you know who this is yet? I'll give you three clues, Baghead: a plastic whistle, a can of Cool Whip, and my girlfriend!

Yeah, you're beginning to get the picture now, aren't you, smart boy? Are you scared? You should be. Yeah, you better be real scared. I can feel you getting scared as you read this. Well, you don't need to know my name. You only need to know that when you mess around with Burt Gooch's girl, you have got some punishment coming.

I'm coming for you, Baghead. The Nameless Dread is coming for you.

You Don't Need To Know (Stuart's Hole, NE)

SARGEANT SCIENCE:

Project #310. Catch a live fly, then drown it
In a glass of common tapwater. When you are
Sure the fly is completely dead, gently take it
Out of the water and sprinkle it with salt. To the
Amazement of your friends, the fly will come to life!

Project #302. If you want your date to put out for
You, slip two aspirins into her soft drink. As the pills
Dissolve, complex chemicals are released which are
Known to stimulate the female sex organs.

"Come on, Willie old pal. Who got you where you are today? Come
on, you know I'm good for it.
Who Really put all those lucrative ideas into your head?
--God borrowing money from Bill Gates

THE CHURCH OF OUR HUMBLE SHEPARD will be celebrating the installation of twelve large stained glass windows created by the Italian artist Pardo Avanti and valued at over one million dollars. These handsome works of art are inlaid with mother-of-pearl and decorated with 24-carat gold leafing. Champagne and caviar will be served in the courtyard for a contribution of only $25. Congregation members only.

NEW STUDIES SHOW THAT ALMOST HALF OF GAY MARRIAGES FAIL
Conservatives point to the Bible

"I'm tired of being told I'm not responsible."

A PROUD AMERICAN . . . . by Elmer Pinkly

The wife and I took one of those European tours last summer. Now, I know the folks in those queer little countries envy us Americans and want desperately to be like us, but I never asked myself the question, why do they fall short? What makes us so much better than them, and why the heck can't they catch up?

Well, the answer came to me all the sudden while we were touring Paris, a city in the country of France . . . . They don't speak American!

It was so simple, and yet so profound, that I had to chuckle. Why had these folks not realized in all the years they've been around that if you want to Be like an American you have to Talk like one? Now I may be a simple fellow from Nebraska, but it seems pretty obvious that you won't be fixed for an American if you're jabbering the French language, which doesn't have a lot of sense to it anyway.

Well, I brought this to the attention of our tour guide, Rene'. I asked him did he like Americans?

"Wee," he said. That's supposed to mean yes.

"Well, then," I said to him. "Do you respect Americans?"

"Of course," he said.

"Then why the heck don't you Talk like an American?" I demanded. "You want to be as good as us, but you don't want to get cracking and work at it, is that the ticket?"

Well, he got all in a lather and went to jabbering a lot of French at me, and throwing his arms all around. I let him simmer down some, then I tried to be reasonable with him.

"Frenchie," I said. "I'm trying to help you out here. How do you plan to Be like an American if you don't speak the lingo? Or if you speak it so it sounds like sissy talk?"

He wouldn't have any of it, and he went off to jabbering again and pounding on his chest the way folks in Europe do when you try to help them. I looked over at my wife and winked. I realized suddenly that these folks would always be second-raters, that jabbering French was too much in their blood.

Well, that's part of the fun of traveling, learning new things. I did have to laugh wondering what my friends back in Nebraska would have to say about a guy with the name of Rene'.

"I don't care who he is, Sandra, I shall fight for your love!"

"Heck, I don't know. One day the boys just started calling me Nevada Joe, and the name just stuck."

A PROPER HOME.....by Helen Bilbo

"Even in the best of marriages quarrels cannot always be avoided. If you have had a little falling out with your husband, bake him one of my Surprise Apple Pies! All you need is a little flour, a quart of fresh apples, some brown sugar, and a dead mouse."

Surprise Apple Pie:
First, bake your crust the regular way (store-bought crust is acceptable), then prepare the ingredients as you always do, using generous helpings of fresh apples and a good sprinkling of brown sugar. Bake the pie to half its time, then remove it from the oven and put it on a good level surface. Now comes the tricky part: gently make a cavity in the exact center of the pie, and insert the dead mouse. Freshly dead mice are recommended. What you want to do now is bake the pie so that the dead mouse becomes crisp enough to be cut with a fork. You'll want your hubby to take several generous bites before he gets the surprise. However, be warned, over-crisping the dead mouse could lead to a telltale odor and give the surprise away.

"FOLKS HAVE NO SENSE OF HUMOR NOWDAYS," complained District Court Judge Roy Mueller, after he sentenced a 12 year old girl to death for shoplifting. "Couldn't they see that it was April 1st?" "Give me a break," the judge said.

AN AFTERNOON WITH THE PHILOSOPHERS . . . by Montrose Peale

The Greek philosopher Plato once said, "I like to have sex with young boys." That doesn't make Mr. Plato any less brilliant, mind you. You have to acknowledge his genius, because he was smart.

But maybe, just maybe scrolls were lost in the flames of the Alexandria Library that demonstrated that he had his head up his ass on most issues. That's right, I dare touch the third rail and suggest that Plato had his head up his ass, and other Hellenic asses as well.

There's a highbrow intellectual assumption out there that we modern folks don't measure up to the great philosophers of ancient Greece. We might not grasp the beauty of Plato's thoughts and insights—but neither do we grasp the hineys of young boys and then bugger them in the forum.

We in the modern world (with the exception of Catholic priests), would hesitate to bugger a young boy. Buggering young boys isn't yet the fashion it was in your day. Yes, yes, I know. There are multitudes of glasses-wearing intellectuals who study you all the time and kiss the ass of you, as if you weren't some primeval monkey that shat and pissed out of a toga.

You launched the Age of Reason, okay I'll give you that. I'll tell that to the young boys you buggered, Plato.

"You remember when you were little and your mom would make you eat a dead rat?"

Cornfield Johnny's Dog Joke of the Month:
How long does it take a flying dog to order breakfast?
I don't know. How long does it take a flying dog to order breakfast?
Well, friend, he can't order breakfast, because dogs can't talk!

Fishing was his life. He loved to fish, and he spent all his time fishing. And then one day...."

From the Unpublished Journal of Sherlock Holmes:

I saw the white sticky substance on her lips. A subtle grey hue indicated that it was spoo delivered by an individual who had recently climbed mountains in east Africa.

I looked over at Watson, who was fixing me with a stupefied stare. I realized suddenly that this young woman had given a blow job—quite recently—to none other than Professor Moriarty.

"I trusted an elf once."

we call that a hornets nest.

My boring cousin Lars, from Sweden, was curious about everything In America.

THE DEVIL AND GEORGE WILL:

"Perhaps nothing ever created by a tragically fallible mankind can equal the sport of baseball, with its nostalgic summer form, its pure economy of motion, its timeless flow—"

"Oh, come on, George. You're a smart guy. Baseball sucks. Deep down you know it, you sense the truth when it touches your spine: George? In the dark of the night? Baseball sucks."

". . . . well indeed. But even you are entitled to an opinion. Can you explain your opinion, Satan?"

"It's not a sport, George, it's a spitting, nose picking, rear end scratching lounging around play with my balls lesson in disgust. By the way, let's change the rules every year why don't we. Let's make sure all the records in the baseball books have little grammatical butt holes next to them. He broke Babe Ruth's record, but-he tied Ty Cobb's record, however-a real sport, George, doesn't qualify every damn record. Grammatical butt holes in the record books means they changed the game. A real sport stays pure."

"Interesting. You've presented an opinion in your usual evil and indelicate way. And your point is-surprise-somewhat well taken. At some point in the life of baseball, things did indeed begin to go wrong-"

"The Designated Hitter."

"You might well be correct-" (Will remembers that he is arguing with the devil)- "But you may also be prematurely morose. You criticize baseball because it has changed. Yet change itself is, after all, the defining theme of America. It can be argued that the game is more electric now, that all the changes have not dimmed . . . . what?"

The Devil is staring deep into George Will's soul. "You can't believe, my good and intelligent friend, that the spectacle of gross men in pajamas blowing snot out of their noses qualifies as a sport."

"Be gone, Demon! You were never my friend."

"The crotch rubbing? George, the spitting and nose picking?"

"They are consummate athletes, the immortal knights of summer, performing that ageless drama of—"

"The ass scratching? George, the ass scratching?"

"Be gone, Demon! I listen to you not!"

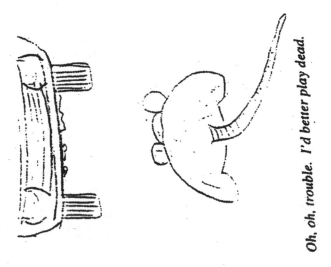

Oh, oh, trouble. I'd better play dead.

TENNESSEE COACH ACCUSES CORNHUSKERS OF "WITCHCRAFT"!
Claims NU players were seen wearing "Demonly Amulets"
and "Holier Twigs". Tennessee State Assembly agrees
to look into allegations.

From the best-selling novel
"Bags to Riches" by J.D. Baghead....

I was approaching the money drawer when the old woman suddenly appeared, blocking the way. She was tiny and fragile, like a piece of fine china, but her eyes blazed with righteous fire.

"Stop where you are, you Boodler!" she cried. "You have swindled this poor family out of all their money, and you're not going to get away with it!"

She was obviously unaware that I had been studying karate. Summoning my energies, I took a deep breath then lashed out, kicking the old woman savagely in the stomach. She crumpled immediately and fell gasping and lurching to the floor. I had to step over her to get to the money, but I could see the fight was out of her.

"I Will get away with it," I said. "Because I swindled them in a clever manner, and it can never be proved. You'll be hearing from my lawyer," I added.

FUN THINGS TO DO IN NEBRASKA--

"Oh, Marcia, it was an April Fools Day joke. I was just kidding. You don't actually think I'd have an affair with your husband!"

CORNFIELD JOHNNY'S COMEDY TIPS:

1. Don't ever use your comedical talents to make fun of people who ain't as smart as you are. Retards have feelings too.

2. Don't ever surprise your audience. Humor has to be predictable or it don't work. They see a pie on the table and a banana peel on the floor, man that pie had better wind up on somebody's face. And every professional will agree, somebody better slip on that banana peel. Unpredictable things just ain't funny, the loud fart in church being one exception to this rule.

3. I advise all young comedians to have two of their front teeth pulled. If you look funny, you're halfway there.

4. And last: stay away from jokes about going to the bathroom. I ate a pile of crab legs at the Big Swede's All-You-Can-Eat Crab Legs Night, and afterwards I attacked the can like it was Pearl Harbor and my rear end the Japs. My whole gut system like to burst out of my behind, and I had cramps like only a woman should get. I sat on the can for an hour and a half, and let me assure you, there was nothing funny about it.

J.D. BAGHEAD SUES THE CITY

Famed Editor John David Baghead has filed suit against the city of Grimpebbet after town Fathers referred to Mr. Baghead as, "A filthy, scummy, dishonest, hateful, dirty-minded, sly conniving little criminal."

"They will have to prove in court that I'm sly," Mr. Baghead stated.

```
;;;;;;;;;;;;;;;;;;;;;;;;;;;;;;;;;;;;;;;;;;;;;;;;;;;;;;;;;;;;;;;
;                                                             ;
; Barbwire, invented in the mid 19th Century,                 ;
; was originally called "Owl Goddamn It!" Wire.               ;
;                                                             ;
;;;;;;;;;;;;;;;;;;;;;;;;;;;;;;;;;;;;;;;;;;;;;;;;;;;;;;;;;;;;;;;
```

J.D. Baghead speaks out . . . .

My opponent in the race for mayor of Grimpebbet recently suggested that it would be inappropriate for me to seek office, because, as the editor of the Grimpebbet Almanac, I may fail the temptation to dishonor myself and let the one duty affect the other. That I might use the great power I have to gain a dark and ungentlemanly advantage in the political world. I can only say that such a suggestion is below comment.

Now let us consider the source of this slander; it is Dr. Alvin Hurlbut. He slanders me because he wants to be major himself.

Will you vote for Hurlbut because he graduated from Harvard Law School? Well, he did practice law for awhile. Then a strange thing happened to our eccentric friend; he found himself tiring of his career in the law, so he just chucked it. Went off to study medicine at Johns Hopkins. He got out and worked as a heart surgeon for a spell, then- well, you know the rest. Now he doesn't want to be a heart surgeon after all, he wants to be mayor of Grimpebbet. The man who couldn't stand the pressures of a law practice of the pressures of the operating room now expects to take on the pressures of major.

He flings at me the charge 'conflict of interest'. Let me explain that. It is a term lawyers are fond of using. It's latin. And it means in this case that Hurlbut feels I may use the Grimpebbet Almanac to stand up to his game. Not unless you make legitimate news, my friend. If you haven't done things you're deeply ashamed of, Hurlbut, then you should not fear the light of day.

Let us say Dr. Alvin Hurlbut is seen at the bar every day drinking and smoking cigarettes in public. Such things are news, my friends, and I won't fail in my duty as a newsman. If Hurlbut swears on the Sabbath, for example, or runs his hands over the naked body of a 14 year old patient simply because it gives him evil pleasures- I'm sorry, but the public should know.

Let us give an example: suppose it was brought to my attention by several honest and trustworthy citizens that Dr. Alvin Hurlbut gained a law degree in order to cover up a life of crime, and that he then diabolically obtained a medical degree in order to skillfully commit his favorite crime, namely murder. An illusion of respectability is the goal of all great criminals.

That if overwhelming evidence came to my attention that Dr, Alvin Hurlbut had indeed murdered several dozen people in cold blood   if such horrors came to my attention, would I fail to inform people? I would not. My duty as editor of the GA would not permit me to help cover up Dr. Alvin Hurlbut's crimes.

Is that conflict of interest? Of course not. It is the natural overlapping of responsibilities. Several of hurlbut's closest colleagues told me straight out that he is nothing but a piss ant. Would I report that in the GA? No, I would not. That's not news, it's gossip. There, hurlbut, is the difference.

I would ask the good Hurlbut, who can't seem to make up his mind what he wants to be, if they did not teach him at Harvard the difference between an editor and a mayor. And what, dear hurlbut, will you want to be once you are major? When the first blush of power fades, when you're faced with pressure, will you then want to be a rocket scientist or professional wrestler?

You had a chance to help people, you were a surgeon. God gave you the skills to save lives. But you don't want to save lives, do you? You want power-power for yourself and the devil with anybody else. I don't know what I can think of a man who can save lives but decides public attention is more important.

I must remind you also, my slippery friend, that your last name ends in the word "butt". Did it ever occur to you that the decent people of Grimpebbet may be traumatized and mortified each time they speak of the major and have to say the word "butt"? Was it ever taught to you that a public figure should never embarrass the public? Not at Harvard, apparently.

You could have changed your name. I've done it several times, it's not that difficult. But you weren't thinking of the decent people you would presume to lead. Sir, you have already proven yourself guilty of slander and pissantry. I won't go any further than that—I only hope a certain 14 year old girl is recovering. You, Sir, have to live with yourself. I pity you, my dear hurlbut, I do.

VOTE JOHN DAVID BAGHEAD MAYOR!!

"Novice George Bush, you will now drop your robes, bend over the Rock of Roald and receive a spanking from the Sacred Spanking Board. Following each spank you will cry out, 'One more, please! One more for Yale!'"

"Novice John Kerry, remove the Sacred Spanking Board from the Ceremonial Sheath, strip naked, place the Horns of Hamish upon your head and administer the Initiation."

--why Skull and Bones never divulge their secrets

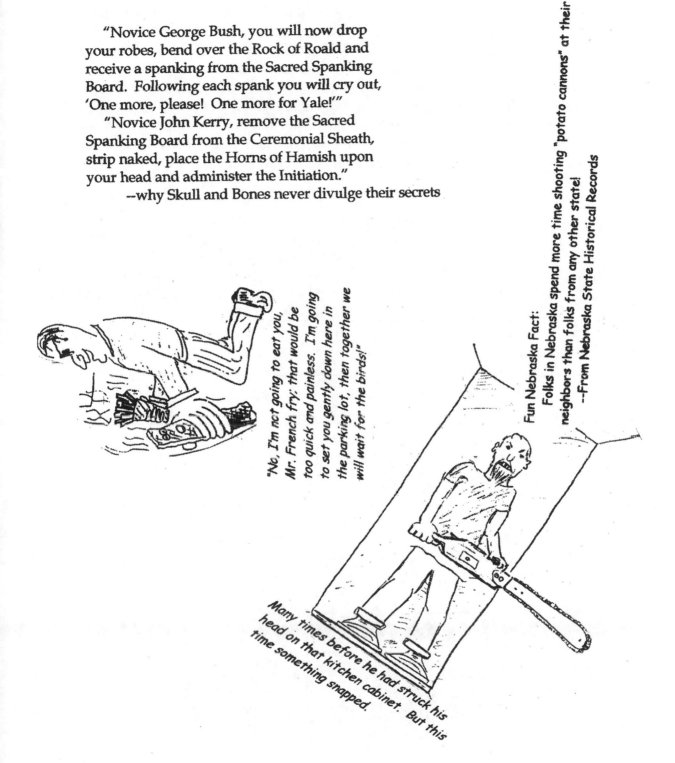

"No, I'm not going to eat you, Mr. French fry; that would be too quick and painless. I'm going to set you gently down here in the parking lot, then together we will wait for the birds!"

Fun Nebraska Fact:
Folks in Nebraska spend more time shooting "potato cannons" at their neighbors than folks from any other state!
--From Nebraska State Historical Records

Many times before he had struck his head on that kitchen cabinet. But this time something snapped.

One final word, Beloved Friend who is reading this: we believe that you will appreciate the quality and high production standards of this almanac. We believe this because you are on a very short list of individuals to receive a free copy. That means you're not only special in our book, you are exceptionally special. That means that we admire your intelligence, basic guts and general astuteness.

We only sent this almanac pro bono to individuals we agreed would spot quality and further our goals. We didn't let the dumb asses in on it. Not yet. You're smart, and so are we, so let's be candid: most of the dumb ass total idiot shitheads you see on the street couldn't even—well, let's not mince words—they're not quite astute enough to understand quality thought.

But you Do understand, we know, that the Grimpebbet Almanac Is quality, that it wouldn't tolerate amateurish art work any more than it would tolerate unfocused reporting. Once again, You understand. That places an artistic and intellectual obligation in your court. You have been blessed with intelligence, and that's more than most folks have. That means that you should promote the Grimpebbet Almanac. Tell your well-to-do friends about it. If they are rich and influential and astute and intelligent, they'll find a way to get the Grimpebbet Almanac out to the—other folks. And if they're merely rich, that's all right too.

At any rate, please call us and tell us what you think of this quality publication. And let us know if you'd like a copy of the Grimpebbet Almanac Issue #2. Contact us at (402)560-4153. Don't worry, it's a secure line. Like all responsible businesses, we have a lackey in the government.

James Howerton
6500 SW 126th St.
Denton, NE 68339
Email: jms.hwrtn@gmail.com

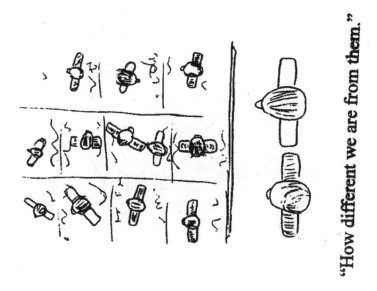

"How different we are from them."

The GRIMPEBBET ALMANAC

Issue #2

Grimpebbet, Nebraska's most trusted publication.

(We care for no one that we might care for everyone)

EVERYTHING YOU WANT IN A NEWS MAGAZINE:

Celebrity Gossip!

"Some Hollywood movie stars sleep with people they're not married to!"

Controversy!

"We believe children Should smoke!"

Racy Language!

"When maggots poop, it comes out you!"

NUDE PICTURES!

A QUICK WORD FROM OUR EDITOR, J.D. Baghead:

Beloved Friends, I'll be brief. Economic realities have made it clear to the Grimpebbet Almanac that we will have to ask you to make certain monetary sacrifices (as we've had to, God knows), in order to remain our Beloved Friends. To break it to you gently, we will explain it to you in French: "Parley vous francey amigos mucho raiseoso the priceo of each issuette."

You see, in the beginning there was the GA #1, forty pages, give or take I believe. Our advertising covered very little of the expense of that, less than one percent. Without really calculating the cost of producing such a masterpiece (criminal postage rates, license fees to the goddamned Federal Government the goddamned Republicans promised to get off our backs—other things, ink, pencils, booze prostitutes- the list really goes on), we settled on the stooge-worthy sum of five dollars. Then one day our Chief Accountant informs us that it's costing us 8 dollars to produce every GA we sell at 5 dollars. Hmmmmm.

I remember well the grunts of satisfaction when some very stupid staff member suggested five dollars per GA. Approval went round the table, because these same staff members buy their beer at less than five dollars a 12-pack. There is something solid and comforting, something inherently good about an honest 5 dollar bill. George Washington on the front and all that. The words "5 dollar bill" touched my staff members like a wizard's wand. As if 5 dollars would even cover sending the goddamn thing out in the mail.

Had I not been thinking about internet porn at the moment, I would have quickly done the math and spotted the disaster. It did occur to me to present the suggestion that not all people who read the GA will pay for it.

No, no, no, no! That's not going to happen! My staff exclaimed. People are good and decent, they won't steal the GA!

Now that polls have shown that over 90% of the people who read the GA do indeed steal it . . . well, dear friends, let's do the math together: We break even at 8 dollars an issue, that is If all issues that are read are legally paid for, and this at 5 dollars per issue. Okay, 8 minus 5 . . . . that leaves 3 . . . . okay, carry the one . . . . then divide by . . . . well, it seems plain to us that we'll either have to get more money from our readers, or we will die. The Grimpebbet Almanac, which has skyrocketed to the top of serious American journalism, will have to fold.

Quite frankly, we're tired of being famous and not rich. Fame without money can go piss on an electric fence as far as we're concerned. Send us as much money as you can possibly afford, or the Grimpebbet Almanac will fold. It saddens us to have to say that we're about fed up.

We are going to produce ONE MORE GRIMPEBBET ALMANAC. This is it, though, unless some substantial grubstake comes down the tubes. We're going to call it THE GRIMPEBBET ALMANAC#3. And for the last time we're going to beg and whimper and debase ourselves for money. We will only charge you 30 dollars for the GA #3, but we hope the less foolish among you will take that as a signal to send far more. Our True Fans will know that unless they send every penny they possibly can, the GA will die.

We are simply that desperate.

Now, a word to the vast majority of Grimpebbet readers who do not pay for it, who are not our beloved friends, whom we do not consider fans:

The Federal Government has just informed us that we cannot avoid, prevent or take vengeance against those who read our almanac and do not pay for such privilege. The official from the Federal Bureau of Investigations we spoke to made our situation quite clear when he said, "you sent the stuff out to the public and didn't think they'd steal it- how fucking stupid are you people? Clap your hands three times and I'll give you an ice cream cone, and you can smash it into your forehead."

That indicated to us that our government would not protect us from robbers and bandits and snatch-purses. Nay, it almost seemed that government officials we spoke to had a sense of glee concerning our plight.

Well, there is a Higher Authority—thieves—than the Federal Government. And we call upon that Authority, who is, namely, God.

THOU SHALT NOT STEAL, God said. That means that reading the GA and not paying for it is breaking one of the 10 Commandments. Yes, it is. Don't try that sniveling excuse stuff, it is. Shut up right now—it is—it's the breaking of one of God's Sacred Laws—it is, you bastards! Shut up and listen to us. If you are reading these words at this very moment and you have not paid for them—no, shut up! You're a thief, you have no opinion in this forum. If you are reading these words and not paying for them, then you are categorically breaking one of God's Sacred Laws.

Look, most of you are already breaking the Sabbath one- you think God's going to tolerate the breaking of Two? THOU SHALT NOT STEAL. Remember that, because . . . well, let us give you a notion of what breaking that Commandment means:

You die. Your soul flies upward, toward paradise. You see a magnificent glittering gate of gold and pearls and diamonds, which is, nonetheless, a gate. There is old beloved St. Peter, who is still fuming over that arrogant upstart St. Paul, and is in no mood to tolerate the likes of thieves.

St. Peter knows you stole the Grimpebbet Almanac, but it amuses him to ask your quivering soul: "Did you ever steal?"

"No," your soul lies.

Now St. Peter knows that you're not only a thief (and probably a Sabbath-breaker), but a liar to boot. He'll kick your soul down to Hell before you know it. And there you'll swirl and churn in the Devil's molten lava. That's the Devil, as in Satan, who buttfucks thieves with razor blades.

Your soul is probably your most valuable possession. Don't throw it away by stealing from us. Ask yourselves that most ancient of questions, readers: Do I want my soul to enter the Kingdom of Heaven, or do I want it stuffed into the black flaming toilet that is Hell?

If you are reading this and haven't sent us money, you feel a tingle, don't you? A kind of—unpleasant sensation. That is the black spider of guilt crawling across your eternal soul. Don't let your spirit fall into a melted, cracked-mirror hellworld of magma and periodic razor blades.

90.

More evidence of that terrible madness that struck this city in the 20th Century.

J. Houghton

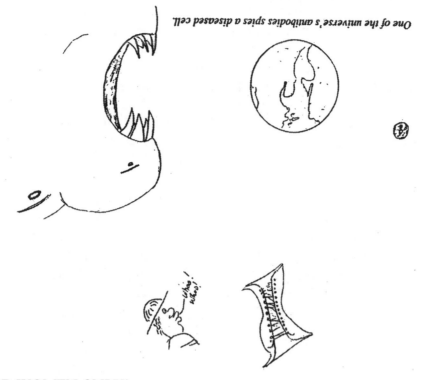

One of the universe's antibodies spies a diseased cell.

THIS AD FOR WOMEN ONLY!

Ladies, now that we're alone, let's be open and honest about our inner feelings—okay? Come on, it'll be fun, you'll see!

Okay, what do we all want more than anything in the world? That perfect hour-glass figure, of course, that ooo-la-la shape that makes men ogle and drool and stare at us. Now I know what you're going to say—But I don't have that shape! I wasn't lucky enough to be born shaped like Marilyn Monroe and other great women of the past! God made me dumpy! I can never have the kind of figure that will make men hoot and say disgusting things to me.

Well, ladies, I have just three little words for you: Yes You Can! And it's as easy as lacing up a shoe.

When you put on my patented TUMMY CHOKER, you'll feel feminine all over, and you'll see a new woman in the mirror, one with the kind of curves men demand. How is this possible? Well, the TUMMY CHOKER is a fashionable undergarment made of the finest Greciean canvas that, when laced around your waist and tightened with the handy adjusting strings, actually chokes out your old figure and replaces it with a knockout display of T and A.

By a process called Mass Transference, cellulose form the bottom of your tummy is relocated downward to the buttocks, giving you that full and rounded hind end. At the same time, you need it most, right into the promised land. Best of all, the unique adjusting strings allow you to adjust the TUMMY CHOKER to whatever pressure (pounds per square inch) you desire!

Order the TUMMY CHOKER now and get absolutely free, the amazing BOOB ELEVATOR!

THE PURPLE AMERICAN ON ASSIGNMENT

I was offered an assignment to attend the conservative Christian Jubilee that was in town and write an article about it. My ultra left wing Liberal friend Adrian Skaggs despised me and grew sick when I told him I was looking forward to it.

"You're going to become one of them," he said. "I've seen it coming with you. It's only a matter of time before you accept Christ."

"Relax," I said. "I'll try to keep you out of Hell. I'll put a good word in."

I thought that was funny. But, it wasn't.

"What do you think you can possibly get out of a Conservative Christian Revival meeting!" he demanded.

"Jubilee," I corrected him. "you never know, Skaggway, you never know." I gave him a naughty grin. "Conservative Christian men might all be boring dweebs, but some of their women are hot. Besides, this is going to be a party! They used the word fun 9 times in their commercial on the Hannity show. Great music, getting down and partying with those well-dressed conservative babes-repressed sexuality, you know. Repressed and unfulfilled. Some of those Conservative Christian babes are divorced, you know, and out combing the field. Damn, I'm looking forward to it! This could be the Happy Hunting Ground."

"You're lost," Skaggs said. "Conservative Christian women —woof! Woof! You've got a sick fantasy, my friend. That's all."

"Typical liberal narrow mindedness," I said. "Go sing Kumbaya at a campfire, Skaggs, I would prefer to pound my flesh into that unpeeled conservative Christian babe who wants me, the Liberal Creep in the ragged blue jeans and dirty tee shirt, to dominate her. No! No! I shouldn't be do9ing this, not with you! No, it's not right! This is fornication! No, I don't do this kind of thing . . . yes! Yes, give it to me! This is so sinful and so naughty that I can't . . . . Oh, yes! Don't stop, you Liberal fuck! Don't stop! Oh, God! Give it to me, Liberal!"

Skaggs had the expression of a vacuum tube. "You are sick. You have sick thoughts, my sad friend."

"I do, and one of them is partying with the Conservative Christians."

"You fool," he said. "Do you think you're going to have fun? Do you think Right Wing Conservatives know how to have fun?"

"I do. I think they will know how to have fun. It might not be my idea of the perfect party, but I'm willing to give them the benefit of the doubt. I want to write an article that's fair and unbiased. In order to do that I've got to really get into the spirit of what they're doing, what this Jubilee is all about. Has it ever even occurred to you that Right Wing conservative Christians might be able to have fun?"

"No."

"The main thing is, if I don't have some Intercontinental ballistic sex with a Conservative Christian girl soon, my fantasy will overwhelm me and I'll die. It's as simple as that, Skaggs."

"See, this sick fantasy has infected your mind. Conservative Christians do not, can not have fun. You should just find a prostitute, pay her a lot of money, and have her dress up like the Conservative girl of your dreams. Have her pretend she's Ann Coulter or something."

"Michelle Malkin," I said.

"Okay. But don't go into this all rah rah. I've seen Conservative get togethers. They're not fun."

I considered the source, Adrian Skaggs, whom the ACLU rejects as being too liberal. So blue the sky hates him.

So, I attended the Jubilee, and now as promised, I'm writing about it. The affair seemed—okay—at first. I resolved going into the auditorium that I would get into the spirit of the thing. I would share the enthusiasm and spirit of all these well-dressed patriotic people. This is an enthusiastic, spiritual crowd, I though! Hey, I don't feel conscious of my wallet as I do at other musical venues. I don't think any of these people are going to rob me. This is great!

To get the party started, a loud country western song suddenly burst out of the great stacks of speakers, a song about God and America and being free.

The crowd went wild, and I thought yeah, Baby, time to Partay! I was right and Skaggs was wrong, there were bunches of Conservative Christian women, some of them no doubt recently divorced, shaking it out there, under flashing auditorium lights. I studied them one by one. That one damn well better be divorced. Yeah, baby!

But time went by, and gradually the patriotic country song shoved and shoved itself into my brain until I feared I would be sick. American flags unrolled on all the walls in striped splendor. Everybody cheered. The loud country song went on and on.

I got control of my gutwork and felt ashamed of myself. Are you against America? Only a blue Liberal worm would get sick at a time like this. If you want to seduce a Conservative Christian chick you're going to have to listen to crappy music.

I thought positive thoughts and went back to studying the conservative women who were shaking their asses nearby. Hmmmm. Okay . . . .

Adrian Skaggs' dark prophecy lurked in my brain. I waited bitterly for the party to show some signs of improvement, and thought it did: the awful patriotic country song faded away, a promise that the fun might now begin.

The first speaker of the night stepped onto the stage, quieted the crowd, and invited us all to join him in the Pledge of Allegiance—with the word God—and we all said the Pledge of Allegiance, and that was fun.

Then came a series of Conservative speakers, and I listened respectfully, but soon distracted myself by looking down the tasteful blouses of the Conservative Christian women nearby. That one's got a bright smile. Temperate, modest, deeply religious. Never had a sinful thought.

It's time you tasted the dark side, my dear. That's right, a creepy sinful dangerous left wing Liberal Lover who unleashes all that pent up guilty repressed Ka-Boom!

I noted that each time a speaker would say "Being Free", the crowd would go wild, and boobs would bounce everywhere. See, I can have fun anywhere, Skaggs! Yeah! I'm having fun here! You, Skaggs, will never have fun until no one dies in Africa.

I kept this courage up for awhile. But I was kidding myself. In the middle of a Christian sermon of all places my predatory instincts warned me that no possible game was here. Things got unfun quickly, and I began looking around to see if there might be booze somewhere, at least beer. This is a party . . .!

I tried getting into the experience, I yelled with everybody else, and louder than most just to show them that I was a hell of a lot more of an American than they were. I threw my arms up with the rest every time a speaker said America or God or "Being Free". But my eyes kept looking for where there might be booze. Maybe this was an alcohol-free event. Of course it was. Conservative Christians don't need booze or drugs in order to have fun. What fool would imagine they would?

Me.

Well, shit, the talk radio host said it was going to be fun, I mean really fun. I shouldn't have expected alcohol, maybe, but when you think of fun you sort of have alcohol in the back of your mind.

I studied the Conservative Christians around me, but could find not one who might even sneak off to the bathroom to share a joint.

Then suddenly another obnoxious patriotic country song came blasting out of the speakers, and the crowd went wild. I had dreaded ever getting the last one out of my brain, now there was this one. I watched the Conservative Christians boogying to the country song and was suddenly in a nightmare. I steadied myself by thinking that things could not get worse than this.

Things got far worse. When the song was finally over, a minister stepped up and began preaching. He led us in a strange tribal chant: Homosexuals—Boo! Godlessness—Boo! Liberalism—BOOOOO!—American—Yaaa!—Values—Yaaa! Being Free—Yaaaaa!

I yelled out too, and jumped around like the rest of them, but I wasn't really having what I could honestly report in an article as being a great deal of fun. These folks were all here to be told what to believe, that was their fun. It was no longer the radio telling them what to believe, this was real!

I went Blue Liberal for a moment, and imagined a naked Liberal woman in candlelight. Skaggs believes in his soul that Conservative Christians can't have fun. That is untrue and unfair. Conservative Christians know how to have fun, it's just not the kind of fun I'm used to.

Oh, hell, it is true. Conservative Christians will have fun the day my butt poops gold. By any sane person's standards, if it is fun, that is what they won't have. I will not give up my fantasy, don't worry, but I understand that it can't happen this night. Not with those barfy country songs attacking my ears. I learned this night what I guess I suspected, that Conservatives can't really have fun, they can only pretend—loudly—that they're having fun. That's probably because fun is a sin, and they're afraid of sin.

There's nothing wrong with that. That's good. I want the Conservative Christian girl I seduce to be afraid of fun. I want her—heh heh—to fear sin. She must be afraid of sin so that together we can help her overcome that fear.

The fantasy remained intact, but this night certainly stepped on my confidence. The well-dressed Conservative Christian babes shaking their asses to the patriotic country song seemed to glare over at me, as if my misgivings were in my eyes. My non-radiant eyes gave me away. It was getting harder to pretend to be a great American, and so I sneaked out of there and into the cold air of the street. I took long deep breaths. I refused to believe that a blue Liberal fag like Adrian Skaggs could be right, even though his prophecy that I would not get laid nor have any form of fun had come true.

But I had been hired by the GA to write about the event, and I think I've given a fair description of it. You, Skaggs, have not triumphed, because my fantasy is stronger than ever. I've learned now how to entrap a Conservative Christian babe. I learned that when you get conservative Christians together, they will become one entity. Together none of them will dare admit to independent thoughts, carnal homosexual scientific or any other. In mass, Conservatives will always behave as one, making it quite impossible to break one of their females out of the herd and have your way with her. Get her alone, that's the key. Away from the herd. Get her to admit that being a Conservative is sometimes—well, all the time—grim and boring, that she needs a break from the damn car radio.

A Conservative Christian girl has to be seduced slowly, slowly. A conservative Christian girl is not going to rip off her blouse for you in a packed auditorium during the Pledge of Allegiance, no matter what your mind urges.

You have to get her alone, away from the group. Cut the ewe from the herd, so to speak. Because the rest of the sheep are safe standing close together, rubbing against each other. But the true kickass American is a wolf. Stick with the theory, my friend: Liberal girls want secretly to be with the sheep-boys, but Conservative girls secretly want to be with the wolf.

"Does that sound sexist?" I asked Adrian Skaggs.

"It's the definition of sexist," he said. "and it shows how sick you've become."

Skaggs was wrong as usual. I had always been this sick.

"As unbelievably sad as it sounds," he said to me. "You let Conservative Propagandists like Michelle Malkin lure you into Conservatism simply with their looks. You don't see a real person, you see an Appearance. And Appearance is one of the weapons Conservatives use. They are All About Appearance, not depth, not substance. Liberals—and no, I'm not afraid to call myself a Liberal!—Liberals aren't interested in Appearance, they want substance."

I pictured Al Franken in my mind. Michael Moore. Ted Kennedy. Skaggs had that one right.

"You forget that Satan, although he doesn't exist, was the most beautiful of the angels," skaggs said. "Take Michelle Malkin's face off the screen, disguise her voice, then really listen to what she says, what she believes."

That was no good. In the case of Michelle, I would find a way to imagine. Anyway, if Adrian Skaggs thought Michelle Malkin was the devil, then he had no business at all to lecture me.

Talk about the utter tragic incapability of having fun.

"In distant times they will remember "The Hookers" as the army I created and led. They will say, "Yes, The Hookers!" and they will remember the deeds of old."
--General Joseph Hooker

"Hey, throw an apple at old Newton and let's see what happens!"
--boisterous British schoolboys

"That antibiotic-resistant bacterium gets all the chicks."

From Bags to Riches
   By J.D. Baghead

   "His arguments were sound, his voice calm and for the moment under control. I had done him a dark injustice and he had called me out to apologize and make amends. I sized him up. He was indeed a small man, with very scrawny arms and a weak chest. Still, he was a man.

   "However, his demeanor indicated to me that he was a meek fellow, all too aware of his frailness. You would charitably call him a pipsqueak. I knew at once that I could pound him and snap him and make him squeal like a pig.

   "How then was I to lower myself to an apology? The crime I committed against him did not seem to hold up against his skinny indignity. He was trembling now, trying to hold courage in those quivering little arms. There was a certain nobility about him that made me angry.

   "His cause was just. I had indeed performed a crime against him. This was many years ago, when I did that sort of thing. He probably would have settled for an apology and not restitution.

   "I took a step toward him, and my suspicions were confirmed when he scampered backward a few steps like a rabbit. I searched his eyes. I saw firmness there, and resolution, maybe even the purity of a cause.

"Now was the time to punch his face in. I did not enjoy pummeling the man, but he had besmirched my honor. It was a fight I would truly have avoided.

"But I could not walk away, I had to fight. That was when it first occurred to me that if I were the mayor of Grimpebbet, I could fight for the people. I could leave the enemies of the people the way I left the pipsqueak, broken and whining out of his shattered jaw. I could fight for the people of Grimpebbet if I were mayor . . . ."

AN OPEN APPOLOGY FROM THE GRIMPEBBET ALMANAC:

We promised you naked girls in this, our second issue, didn't we? We did, we remember, and we're willing to stand up and admit it and to openly apologize for—well—under circumstances quite beyond our control—not having the naked girls like we promised, splayed out and all that.

Okay. No splayed out beautiful naked girls. But you've opened this Almanac, and there's no going back. What is important now is that you paid for this almanac and didn't steal it. Leave us remind you, Beloved Friends, that if you're reading these words then you've already cracked our magazine open. We know that you bought the issue. We trust and pray that if you're this far into the great reading you haven't violated Federal Law and enjoyed this issue without paying for it.

Please, please don't undermine our belief that we're all decent, generous Beloved Friends, willing to roll up our sleeves and pay our own way. America can't have fallen so far down that people will not pay honest money for honest work. The GA cannot believe that; and no matter how far you Commies push us, we ain't gonna give up on America. So what do you think about that, Communist thieves that steal the Grimpebbet Almanac and make copies to give to your thieving little Communist friends, and then laugh in our faces not ever having paid us a dime? What do you think about that? We won't abandon America. No, crooks, it ain't a gonna happen. Steal from us like a skulking loser if you have to—but Fella, we're not going to give up on America.

Enjoy the Grimpebbet Almanac and not pay for it and you're not an American. You're some kind of . . . we don't know what you are. Okay, this is the last thing we're going to say: If you paid us the legal price for this publication, if you are indeed a "Beloved Friend", then our only wish is that you enjoy it to its fullest, that you take all the wisdom and courage from it that you can.

If you did not pay for this issue, we hope this almanac makes you choke and get sick and vomit on your spouse, and gives you ringworm and a violent case of the runs.

My son is in junior high, and he came up to me the other day and said he wanted to talk to me about something. He said that he was having these thoughts about his English teacher, Miss Evans, that he had even thought about her vagina. And I patted him on the back and said, "Join the crowd, Son."

Burned at the stake for Witchcraft
--Mary Sinclair, servant girl
them with proper hygiene."
tiny as to be invisible to our eyes, and that we may fight
sweeping the colonies must be caused by parasites so
to no other conclusion than that these diseases that are
"I have thought long and hard about it, and can come

Famed Televangelist James Van Hagee Speaks Out For Abstinence:
"My wife and I have practiced it for years, and it makes for a good, spiritually sound marriage."
"Yes......it does," Mrs. Van Hagee agrees.

"What makes me such a handsome and dashing specimen of a man? It is because I am racially pure."
--Heinrich Himmler

"We felt that, given the situation in Europe at the time, in order to introduce our unique culture to the western nations in an effective manner, it behooved us to kill all their men, rape their women, make slaves of their children and burn their societies to the ground."

--Ghengis Khan, a memoir

I didn't have to chew if off, I had the keys to the handcuffs. But that Would have been the coward's way out.

The commander takes an enemy hill.

Manfred realized suddenly that his carefully thought-out plan was not working.

 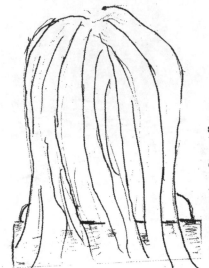

"Miss Arnold, as a Doctor of Psychology,
I understand the close connection between
The mental and the physical; therefore I think
I should do a pelvic exam."

RHODE ISLAND: "Land that time forgot."

NEW MEXICO: "A bleak desert, but look at the sunset!"

ARIZONA: "Hotter than a motherfucker in the summer."

CONNECTICUT: "Land of (wink wink), Old Money."

ILLINOIS: "Abraham Lincoln? Ulysses Grant? Chicago? What more do you pussies want from us?"

INDIANA: "We have a car race."

ARKANSAS: "You'd better jump your sister while she's still got her teeth."

Our only interest in the Middle East is to spread Liberty.

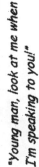

"Young lady, I assure you that the Laws of Gravitation can only be explained if I am allowed to take your breasts into my hands."

—Isaac Newton tries out a new line

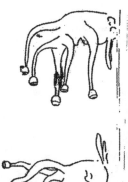

"Young man, look at me when I'm speaking to you!"

46

From the Unpublished Journal of Galileo:

"Seeing in my mind's eye the spectacle of blistering flames consuming my body as I stand helplessly tethered to a post, the hate-filled crowd mocking me and cheering as I scream in unimaginable torment, it came to me suddenly that indeed the earth is the one and only center of the universe."

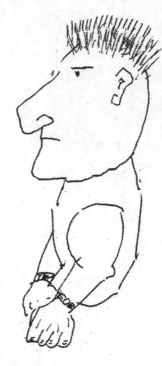

It was a profound and gratifying notion, that Calvin could kick the poop out of everybody else.

"....*now* about that pesky theory that the earth revolves around the sun...."

--Kansas Board of Education

SARGEANT SCIENCE: Idle musings.

...How awesome it must have been when the mighty Tyrannosaurus Rex cut a fart.

...No matter what you say about the Jews, that Einstein was a pretty smart cookie.

...If we do find new life forms in our galaxy, it would probably be a good idea to get rid of them.

....Hey, you bone heads who sat in my class all those years ago and laughed at and made fun of Chemistry, I got one word for you—Viagra.

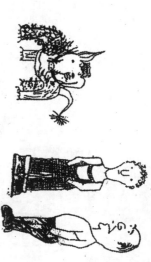

"No, it's not a purebred."

A Grimpebbet editorial:

Bill O'Reilly recently used his powerful tee vee show to take the Grimpebbet Almanac to task for not ridiculing women as savagely as we do men. For giving women a free ride, kissing up to them instead of revealing them as mean spirited and uptight, like we do men.

"Why do you only pick on powerful men, and give women a free pass? He demanded.

To his credit, Mr. O'Reilly even summoned the audacity to invite the whole shit 'n shebang of us onto his show to debate the issue, as if we ever had the courage to do such a thing.

No, but we can create an imaginary interview. We have granted this interview because Mr. O'Reilly is a powerful man who could make things rough for us. And because he feels he has the winning army because it's on the "moral high ground".

Not so fast, B.O. We don't pick on girls, that's true. And, to be perfectly honest, we don't pick on men. We can't honestly accuse you of being puritanical and uptight, because we've never met you, nor your other powerful right wing conservative guy pals. We can't say that because—well, yes we can, because you are! That's because you're all-secretly—heh heh—you know—scared of girls? An early childhood "tightening in the throat" that turned some boys into suits and ties.

Dear Beloved Friends: Before you judge us against the powerful Fox Media, please keep in mind that throughout this imaginary interview, Mr. Bill O'Reilly was stabbing a guilty spoon into a tub of Ben and Jerry's ice cream. We provided the damning evidence ourselves, free of charge—our favorite—Cherry Garcia.

The GA's imaginary interview with Bill O'Reilly:

B.O. "Okay, why don't you ever insult women? Like say Susan Sarandon?"
GA. "The answer, Bill, is, Duh. You expect us to call Susan Sarandon names when all the while we're imagining her in bed, making love to us—"
B.O. "What about Barbra Streisand. Come on."
GA. "Right, who wore the dress in that movie that had the hands clutching those sensational—"
B.O. "Come on. Susan Sarandon? Barbara Streisand? Can you imagine Either of them holding public office?"
GA. "yes, we can. American history has proven that stupid movie stars do better in public office than career politicians. They tend to be less subject to corruption and flattery. Actors and Actresses (John Wilkes Boothe aside), have contributed greatly to our political past."
B.O. "Come on. Give me a break."
GA. "our polls have shown that, Bill. And the GA backs up everything we say with proven scientific polls. They may not always be true, but they are fair and they are balanced."
B.O. "Okay, forget movie stars. What about the Dixie Chicks?"
GA. "What about them. A fantasy beyond the imagination. We don't care if they're Communist."
B.O. "Oprah Winfrey? Come on."
GA. "You gotta be kidding, B.O. Make fun of a goddess? Don't you sense the unrealized sexual Armageddon inside that gorgeous package? All those decades of overachieving, unrequited—"

B.O. "Okay, okay, I get your point."

GA. "You're talking decades of pent up Gold Coast multi-billionairess workaholic hormonal energy that has grown into enormous sexual proportions!"

B.O. "Okay, I see where this is going. I get your point."

GA. (sensing advantage) "Well, if you get our point, Sir, then why the harassment and criticism? Your threatening posture has been noted. We only suggest that if you can't fall in love with Oprah Winfrey then obviously something happened to you on the playground, long ago. Something twisted you."

B.O. "Okay, enough. I'm not twisted. You guys are the ones who are twisted. Okay, you're being jokesters, I can dig that —"

GA. "No, Bill, we're not. We're deadly serious. If you don't harbor some deep fantasy about Oprah, you are simply not human, and we feel sorry for you."

B.O. (almost laughing) "Okay, come on, fellas, we all get your point, lame as it is. You don't want to have a serious discussion with me, fine."

GA. "B.O., you're asking us why we don't pick on girls. Let us ask you this: Why do you pick on girls? Why, B.O.?"

B.O. "Okay, let's break for the commercial. Nice talking to you guys."

GA. (wants desperately to get in a snotty last word, but suddenly realizes that even imaginary interviews need commercial breaks, a fact the seasoned O'Reilly uses cleverly against them).

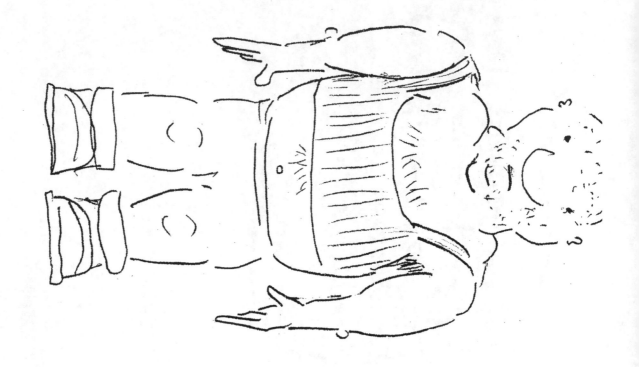

I'm sorry, Mr. Petrocelli, but ballet requires a certain lightness of form.

The strongest geometric figure rubs it in.

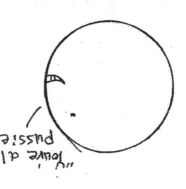

"You're all pussies!"

Farmers gang sign.

"APRIL IS THE CRUELEST MONTH"

Know what poem that line came from? If you don't, then you're ... uneducated fool.

But you don't have to stay that way. You see, the classics aren't as mystical as those snooty literature professors want you to believe they are. Can a truck driver quote Shakespeare? Hell yes, he can!

How?

With Audio Cassette Tapes Digests of the World's Great Works of Literature!

Why take the time to actually read those boring and confusing old books that intellectual society demands you to read? Wouldn't it be easier to simply plug in one of our handy tapes and let stars like Barbra Streisand and Whoopi Goldberg read the condensed versions of those boring—yet socially valuable—works of literature?

Won't people be impressed when you quote Goethe, Cervantes and Tolstoy? They will take away forever the valuable impression that you have read these titanic geniuses. Your confidence will soar like Poe's raven and your self-esteem will shine like the hood of Gatsby's car, or we will cheerfully refund your money.

"I am a vegetarian. I abhor the killing of animals. I neither drink alcohol nor do I smoke tobacco. I abstain from sex and encourage hard work, dedication, and loyalty. I believe one should live a clean, productive and healthy life."

--Adolph Hitler

53

The GA's Advice to All English Majors:

Kids, stop worshipping those freaky foreign writers and support the writers from your own country. Carl Sandburg sensed it, we Americans have our own great-shouldered and full-bodied brand of fiction. Our fiction is beefy and robust, and so much of foreign fiction is—well, Adventures of the Saucy Queen type stuff, if you get my drift. The effeminate rogue with the sharp wit and clever word plays who is insufferable but rarely funny. We have our own confident and muscular style of fiction, so screw you, Britain. And you too, France.

Put William Shakespeare in the ring with old Papa Hemingway. Slap some gloves onto the hose-wearing Brit. No, not silk women's gloves, boxing gloves! Then shoo his little butt into the ring. I guarantee you Hemingway would lay that skinny ass playwright out in a New York minute. Send out that fat French guy who wrote all the novels. Send him out against—say, Edgar Allan Poe. I don't know quite how, but I do know that E.A. Poe would find a way to topple the gross Gaul. Because America has come into her own, and American writers know how to kick ass.

Foregn writers who try to compete against Americans inevitably get their asses kicked. Alfred Lord Tennyson, spoiled little fairy who never worked a day in his life—he's going to last in the ring with tough old Walt Whitman? I don't think so. One round and Whitman would have himself another submissive bed mate.

Voltaire? A witty, clever boy. All right, put the pretty little fellow in the ring with Robert Louis Stevenson and let's see what happens. French toast, that's what happens. The Nobel Prize for Literature? What a sad joke. Just because it's South American and boring and the .02 percent of people who read it don't understand it, doesn't automatically make it Literature. Hey, Nobel Prize Committee—come onto our turf and try to pull that shit. Stop being an inclusive, politically correct introspective cowardly United nations mass of worms and smell the coffee: Americans write better than everybody else, just as we do everything else better than everybody else.

You'll not bring your squiggly little Nordic butts around the vicinity of Nebraska, will you? Because you know damn good and well what the Grimpebbet Almanac bunch would do to you. Faster than a speeding bullet you'd get your butts ripped open for not giving us the prize and the money when even a blonde haired empty-minded Swede knows we deserve it. Yeah, you ain't showing your faces anywhere near Nebraska, USA, are you? Nobel Prize, my ass, Gunther. How 'bout we put Stephen King on your asses?

*(This advice paid for by the NEBRASKA CHAPTER OF THE STEPHEN KING FAN CLUB)

TRUE TITLES OF THE CLASSICS:

"How Black was my Valley"—the true story of a Welsh coal
Mining community.

"It Ain't a Yearling No More, and it's Time to Butcher the Damn Thing"—the true story of
a boy and his pet deer.

"WAR AND—page after pager after page of never ending prose
That is so boring and mind-numbing you finally begin skipping pages, then whole blocks of
pages—PEACE".

"Piglet"—the true story of a Danish prince so whiny and snively that it's a miracle he is
considered tragic.

"Gone with the Dumb Ass Idea to Start a War"—the true story of Scarlett and Rhett.

From the Unpublished Journal of Socrates:
"Though I am hard of hearing, I believe they said
they would serve me herbal tea in the morning. Then
at last I will write about all I know."

"I don't know a great deal about
these grizzly bears, Lord Snow—
however, we used to frighten away
the European brown bears by jumping
up and making menacing noises..."

Experts In Paranormal Studies Analyze Data in the Field:

"They're entities all right. Look at the plasma readings I'm getting. They're entities, and they Must be supernatural. Can we agree on that?"

"Of course. Could they be demons?"

"Hard to tell at this point, but I wouldn't be surprised if some of them are, so watch your step."

"But look how the needle is moving, up and then down. Something more is going on here."

"These are ghosts we're dealing with—that's what you're saying?"

"Of course they're ghosts, I assumed you knew that already. No, something stranger than ghosts, something—"

"Alien ghosts!"

"My God, you might have—yes, you have to be right. Such a strange configuration of plasma forces. How the needle moves up and then it moves down—they have to be the ghosts of alien beings, there's no other explanation."

"They're the ghosts of aliens, we can't doubt that. But there's even something more bizarre going on here. This can't be all of it."

"Alien ghosts from another Dimension!"

"I was just about to suggest that. Look how the needle moves up and down. These are Alien Ghosts from another Dimension. Do we all agree?"

"Agreed."

"Yes—agreed—but this can't be all."

"No, but we've come about as far as we can without doing more research on this. We have to ask ourselves some pretty complex questions now: From what dimension did they come? How did they die once they reached Earth? What are they trying to tell us?"

"Well, we will just have to start at the beginning and work our way through this."

"Right. The Mothman Files. Let's get started . . . ."

Farmer Adolph Hitchcock was pulling an old plow across the campus of the University of Nebraska when his vintage John Deere tractor began losing compression.

He unhooked the plow and left it there, then drove the tractor home to his garage. When he returned for the plow, he found to his astonishment that it had drawn national attention and was considered one of the ten best campus sculptures in the world, and that artists were flying in from every nation to see it.

After selling Plow on Campus to the university for half a million dollars, farmer Hitchcock quickly signed a deal with the New York Metropolitan Museum of Art to purchase other works: *Baler in Barn, Mower in Garage, and The Tractor Lisa.*

The Balloonman's blind date
Did not look promising.

"No, God did not create man from the river, nor woman from the clouds. That's ridiculous. God created man from the dust, and woman from the Rib of man."
—a missionary teaches the savages

When I said I wanted John the Baptist's head, I didn't mean That head
—Salomi!

FARM WISDOM . . . . .
Those spent herbicide and pesticide containers
Don't have to be taken to an expensive dump site
Or tossed out the back of the truck on some lonely
Road. Cut the plastic tops off them and use them
For handy containers. You can haul anything from
Dogfood to drinking water in them, and as they are
Made from plastic, they will last forever.

"I want you to teach my boy how to fight! I don't want him to have to take any lip from anybody!"

"Random Notes To Me" . . . . by Dr. Michael Savage:

1. Invite people to talk about issues, then immediately interrupt them and run your mouth off and give your opinion and run your mouth off until time is up for this caller—then hang up and talk some more.

2. Encourage listeners to call you "Doctor", even though . . . well, anyway, give a free copy of your book to every caller who refers to you as "Doctor".

3. Use good old days stories to show listeners you're not a miserable phony. Tell a good old days story every week. Make them think you have a warm and compassionate side.

4. For God's sake keep the Christians on your side. Mel Gibson proved it for all time, there's a lot of Christian money out there. And man are they gullible.

5. Call the listeners The Savage Nation, that way they'll believe they're—like cultural warriors. Make them believe they're more intelligent than everybody else, even though they're so stupid you have to interrupt them and keep them from talking.

6. One Rule: You can disagree with me, but if you insult me I'll hang up on you, you red diaper doper baby homosexual vile Mexican Arab piece of garbage.

7. Remember, you're the genius here. Dr. Savage is the genius. You're the one—remember?—who Albert Einstein patted on the back and said "Yes, Mike, I do believe in God."

8. Invite people to call in and disagree with you—or agree with you—then interrupt them and give your opinion until time runs out, then hang up the phone.

9. Remember that even though you're the greatest writer who ever lived, you insulted the left wing homosexual media, and it mobilized its evil publishing army to keep your book from being a best seller. You see what happens when you don't buy my book, members of the Savage Nation? The left wing liberals win, they take over, they turn our society into a gigantic San Francisco—that's what will happen if you don't buy and read my book.

10. Okay, here's a free copy of my book . . . .

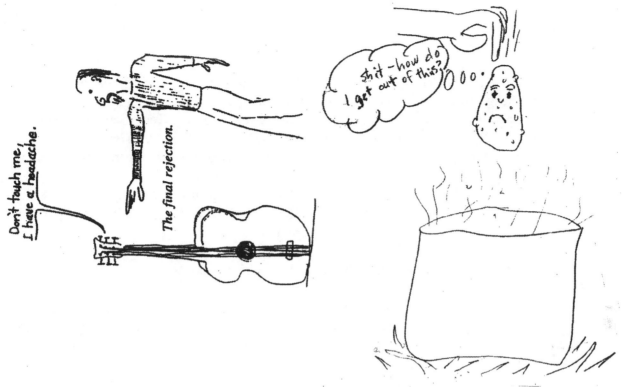

The final rejection.

Too late the potato achieves awareness.

Heinz performs an ill-advised practical joke.

A PROUD AMERICAN . . . . by Elmer Pinkly

By now you've heard about those crop circles they found out south of Pleasant Dale on the Silas Mockingbird farm. I went out there myself and had a look, and let me tell you, they were eerie, man. Bob Price, who teaches drafting at the Squigmy Tech School, said they were "geometrically perfect", and no human could have made them. And Nimrod Heckler, who speaks Italian, claims he's almost sure the strange markings inside the circles is ancient Egyptian writing.

So I decided to call in an expert and see what's really going on out there. I called Dr. Lieberman at the university there in Lincoln. He's supposed to be some kind of expert on Astronomy. Wouldn't you know it, he had a German accent.

"Give me your opinion on these crop circles out there by Pee Dale, Doc," I said.

He hesitated, the way a German will do, to show he's better than you and you're taking his time.

"I'm sure it iss a joke, Mr. Pinkly," he finally said.

"A joke." Well, I gave him a little pause of my own, just to show him an American can do it too. "Have you seen these things, Doc?" I pursued. "Have you studied them?"

"No, uff course not," he said, all sausage and sour kraut.

"I see. Well, I've seen them and I have studied them, and you'll have to excuse me if I mistook you for a professor of Astronomy."

"I am a professor uff Astronomy," he said.

"Then why don't you get cracking and put a study to those things," I said. "It seems to me that other life forms wouldn't be landing their craft near Pee Dale if there wasn't something attracting them there. You want to find out what, don't you?"

I had to explain this to a university professor?

"You make a joke? This iss a joke, eh?" He gave me one of those beerhall chuckles.

"I'm not joking, Adolph," I said. "My readers want to know what the heck is going on out there!"

"I do not beleef little green men have visited Nebraska," he said.

I knew he was sneering. The way he said 'Nebraska' made it certain that he didn't believe we were as cultured as Berlin and Munich.

"Let me ask you this, Adolph," I said. "Do you beleef that people came from monkeys?"

Well, he spooted and clucked and tried to change the subject the way eggheads will do when you try to pin them down. I'd had about enough of this Teuton.

"You beleef that people came from monkeys, but I don't see any monkey-people. I did see those crop circles, Adolph, and-"

"Herman," he corrected me. "My name iss Herman, please."

I had to stop and grit my teeth. Only my professionalism kept me from losing my cool.

"I'm an experienced reporter," I said. "You don't think I can tell when somebody's trying to duck the issue and cover up things?"

"There iss nothing to cover up, Mr. Pinkly! It iss a practical joke, these circles in the field! An old joke, ha ha!"

Now I'd pushed the right buttons. The jackboots came out and I had a real Siegfried on my hands.

"You'd probably spill the truth if you were talking to another Fritz, wouldn't you?" I charged.

The line went dead after that, and it's just as well. I've learned that you can never get a straight answer out of a scientist. I do know one thing, you'd have to be pretty lame to beleeef those crop circles were made by humans.

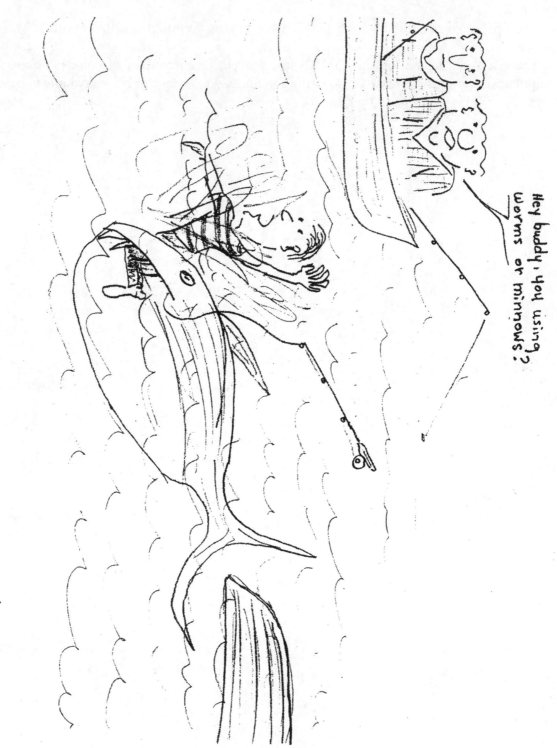

INTERMISSION,

This is the Intermission Page, a time to sit back, take a deep breath and absorb the wisdom of the GA #2, part one. Yes, it's true, we have become more gentle and understanding. One might even say some of the views expressed in our previous issue would be deemed cynical and inappropriate compared to our present standards. That cynical stuff is over, our Beloved Friends. No more of that for us.

We have studied the Mel Gibson movie and found that they general public is more willing to give you money if you're good and not bad. Therefore, we have resolved not to be bad. We're not going to offend anyone or hurt anyone's feelings ever again, so don't expect it of us.

We ar te Grimpebbet Almanac are justly proud of the improvements we've made to this periodical since the first unfortunate issue which, let us be the first to admit, was a shitty messy failure.

But you remained in our corner, dear friends. And you'll be rewarded with higher quality. Know that we support the FCC's crackdown against indecency, and that we will be the first to report other writers who refuse to stop using vulgar language. We've backed away completely from offending people; we've cleaned up our language. We want to make the GA safe reading for even one of those sad, brain-washed Jehovah's Witnesses.

Clean and Decent, that is the motto we've had painted on the very walls of this institution, in our own blood, by the way. The skunkshit you witnessed in our first edition was awful, and we're ashamed—but it taught us several important lessons about making people angry, and not to.

Other regional almanacs might purposely go out to offend folks, just to make a dollar, but those days are over for us. If you don't believe that, you're a fucking asshole. We want you to send us money for being Clean and Decent, not butthole wipes, like those other almanacs are. Send them money if you want to be offended. We refuse to offend you, because we like you. Around the office we have a nickname for you: Our Beloved Almanac Friends. It doesn't matter if you're a Christian (even one of the real creepy ones), or a Muslim (talk about creepy), a Belgian or a South African or a Secular Humanist (creepiest of all). If you're some stupid European, or an especially unpleasant Russian, we'll like you just the same.

Offending people just isn't funny anymore. We've all grown up. Only a Canadian or a slav or a woman would think that kind of humor is funny. And if South Americans want to learn dirty American words, they'd better just skip us by.

Clean and Decnet. Offend no person. That is the Grimpebbet Almanac from this day forward. And we hope that you'll send us enough money to spread the love and decency our "Beloved Almanac Friends". Deserve. Send as much as you can, please.

Henceforth we will strive to offend no one, not even the bull-headed and subversive Amish who clog the public highways with their god damned horse carriages. No offensiveness, our writers have been warned, or you'll get a write up and a stern talking to from the Editor himself. Clean and Decent, that's our new motto, and we're not ashamed to admit we're proud of it.

We've cleaned up our act and said we're sorry. Let's leave it at that and go on to better and brighter tomorrows.

(To our "Beloved Friends": You're going to find that we've completely cleaned up our language in this issue. New Federal regulations have opened our eyes and frightened us, and we see that vulgarity is no longer the rule of the day. Questionable terms such as cocksucker will no longer appear in the GA, not even for a laugh).

LIFE BEGINS

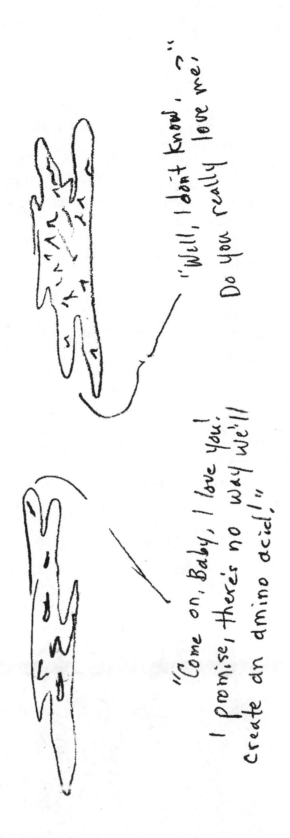

"Well, I don't know...?"
Do you really love me?"

"Come on, Baby, I love you!
I promise, there's no way we'll
create an amino acid!"

Brown paper bags:

From their biography "Our Kamph"

Why do we do what we do? Doo wap a doo . . . . uh, why-how-where-when-what-that's it! What do we do? Well, our goal is to make money . . . . well, not money, per se. Art, that's really our goal, to make Art. God, too many whiskey sours . . . .

Okay. The goal of brown paper bags-okay-it's . . . . the creation of Art, let's get that straight from the git go. Although we use and admire many products (Philips Canadian blend, Marlborough Reds filter king in the box, Busch Beer, Lunchables), we would never consider selling out to those rats who run all the big corporations.

They would have to give us Holee God money to push us into such a shame. Big, enthusiastic megadonish crap and butt loads of hard cash. Believe us, friends, when we say we would never sell out for anything less.

That won't happen, you'll see. Because the corporate clone-fest that rules the world doesn't want you to see that we're about making mo-Art.

I know, I know what you're thinking. Marlborough should pay brown paper bags colossal buckaloids for advertising their fine product.

Come on, you guys. Send us some money so we can continue creating Art. Your product is swell, we admit it. We stop at a U-Stop for smokes, if they don't have Marlborough Reds filter king in the box, well the boy behind the counter gets his head torn off, and we commit unseemly acts in the bloody cavity that was his neck line.

Here's the gist: Send us good quality money, and brown paper bags will endorse your product.

Refuse to send us money, and brown paper bogs will vilify your product and make it look like the stupidest thing on earth. We can—and will—make fun of your relentlessly, Mr. Big Shot Corporation.

We can tell our fans that—is composed of ostrich feces. Little hints like that to our fans—you get the drift.

Think about it, Big Boys.

A Grimpebbet Editorial:

As you know, several famous personalities recently banded together and filed suit against the GA for defamation of character. No, no, don't freak out, we won the lawsuit, it was thrown out before it ever got to the state level. And although we cannot mention any of the names of these celebrities, pending a possible appeal, we can offer our commentary on the entire unfortunate event:

First of all, we would very sincerely like to tell you that we hold no grudges against these famous-people. That forgiveness is the greatest gift, the greatest power in the world, and that if they will accept our apologies, then we will humbly accept theirs.

We would very sincerely like to tell you that, but if you are a Beloved Friend you know that instead we will blacken our hearts with revenge, and seek to attack and humiliate and clean-as in "to clean a fish"—these famous scoundrels who dared file suit against us. It's not enough that they're rich and famous, you see. No, they can only gain fulfillment trying to destroy a helpless and handicapped almanac like Grimpebbet.

It is the nature of fame to begin to despise whatever laughs at it. Well, don't worry, famous schmucks, we're not going to laugh at you ever again—no, that would be too quick and painless, and our monstrous writhing souls are too black with hatred and too thirsty for revenge for you to get off that easy. Now that Freedom of Speech has come up and chomped on your asses, dear tidbits, you'll no doubt go off sulking to France, not even giving a thought to the fact that you pissed off the Grimpebbet Almanac, and they would immediately seek revenge. Fame did not give you invulnerability, the law has seen to that, ha ha. We have Sicilian friends with scars on their faces, and Fame sends them a Christmas card every year.

A United States judge ruled that we have the right to make fun of you. Huh? We can't hear you. You're not criticizing the GA now, are you, peckerwoods? You thought because folks worship you that you had the First Amendment in your pocket, eh? I can say what I want but nobody else can. Well, take another Tums, Fame-oid, because our pal the federal judge just let us off the chain. You're in for it now, big shots. Lawsuit over, slam dunk, you're in a world of shit, guys. Because you got nothing in your pocket but a limp dick.

My God, that you've gone so far and achieved so much, only to be picked on by some odious small town Nebraska dirt rag! Ho ho, that alone must drive you to the liquor cabinet.

Well, it's going to get worse now, tidbits. Yeah, it is. We had all agreed to stop satirizing famous people, because it just wasn't fair. That was until they sued us—and lost! Now we all agree to get revenge in the most terrible manner possible. Our souls are lightless in this matter; not one photon of light penetrates our souls on this one, Fameoids. For you have awakened the demonic ten-headed creature, and you shall pay.

For Kids Only:

Kids . . . . look at poor Baghead, see how skinny he
Is? Fact is, kids, your pal Baghead is starving
To death. You could help, if you really cared—
No, don't send food . . . . you see, Baghead isn't like
Us, he doesn't live on food. Baghead must have money
In order to survive. That funny old Baghead!
But you could help, if you really cared. You've
Written to Baghead before, remember? To get your free
Brown paper bag and your Eddie ring, and the Baghead
Switchblade for only $12.99?
Well, you know it would be fun if you took all the
Paper money out of Mom's purse and all the paper money
Out of Dad's wallet and sent that money to Baghead.
Wouldn't that be a great trick, kids? And we could
Keep it secret—it would be kind of like a secret
Club.
If you don't do this, Baghead will die, and you
Won't ever see him again. There will be no more funny
Cartoons. No more Sergeant Science. No dog joke of
The month. Look at him, kids. Look at Baghead.
It's up to you, kids.

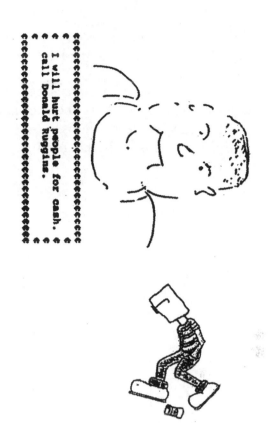

Artist's drawing of what Baghead now looks like

BROWN PAPER BAGS ADVICE TO YOUNG MUSICIANS:

We've always believed that if you're going to do something, do it the way a Tyrannosaurus Rex takes a dump, so the sound is heard by every creature of the forest. In other words, don't hold back.

Let your music spill out and fill the valleys and climb the mountains and scamper down and dive in the ocean and swim around. Don't be afraid of people laughing at you- we went through that long ago, and we got over it. Don't be afraid to be yourself and to not be—to not be . . . . that's right, somebody you're not. People will be mean to you at first. They will mock you and ridicule you and despise and terrorize you, but at some magic moment they will pity you and leave you alone.

Maybe then they'll listen to your music, your words. Maybe they'll unfasten their eyes from the teen bosoms of the latest pop stars and actually listen! To your music! With their goddamn ears!

So they would rather stare at teen bosoms than listen to your songs, that's quite their loss. So they would rather think about teen bosoms glistening hard in white leather tops.

Fringed white leather tops.

Teen bosoms glistening sweaty above cute, winking belly buttons. Yes, teen bosoms . . . .

LETTERS TO THE EDITOR:

Dear Mr. Baghead,

I am 80 years old and confined to a chair, so I spend a lot of time reading, and I appreciate a local almanac that is well-written and entertaining. Your is neither, although I do enjoy reading Tales of the Pioneers and some of the other essays. They remind me of when I was young and folks didn't need drugs and pornography and all this electronic hoolie-poolie in order to get by. And good Christmas everywhere should enjoy the uplifting messages of Pastor Milton Crane. Please give Dr. Crane more space in which to denounce those terrible Mormons and to keep us posted on what the Catholics are up to. And how about a senior citizen discount on your subscriptions?

God bless you.

Mrs. W. Studdwart (Tokyo, NE)

Dear Baghead and Readers,

You all know me, ordinarily I'm the funniest guy on the planet. But when I see people using humor to poke fun and ridicule, well it throws water on my comedical genius a little bit. Such as what happened when you, Baghead, suggested that a certain rancher we both know cried a little too hard when a certain sheep went off to slaughter. That crosses the line, Baghead!

Let me ask you this, B.H. You ever been in love? I mean a real special love. And did you lose that love? I don't care who you are, you're going to shed tears, and there ain't nothing unmanly about it. So let's think about what we're writing, Baghead, and show a little class.

Cornfield Johnny (retired rodeo clown)
Grimpebbet, NE

"The maiden at the lake was beautiful, and I loved her
very much. But no, they said I have to marry my dumb
old sister."
                              --King Tut

Why ghosts cannot masturbate

From the unpublished journals of Thomas Crapper:
"I have just perfected an amazing invention! The world's
first self-sweetening water closet. I daresay it will make my
name famous throughout history!"

"Hi, Bob, I'm Dr. Kovalt and I'll be doing your surgery this morning.
You probably don't remember me, but we went to high school
Together. Little Bernie Kovalt? Boy, you sure gave me a hard
time. Remember when you beat me up and took away my girlfriend?
That was a good one, ha ha."

72

NEWS QUOTES OF THE DAY:

Barbra Streisand: "I'm ashamed to be an American. Every day I order my driver to take the limo through the poor sections of the city. And I ask myself, isn't America the land where dreams can come true?"

Bill O'Reilly: "Don't forget, you only have twenty more days till Christmas, so get your order in for the NO SPIN ZONE ear muffs. They're going fast . . . ."

Michael Moore: "There's a terrible and distorted historical myth that Americans won their independence by using guns."

Alan Colmes: "We could all get along, couldn't we? We could listen to one another and find common ground. We could be more moderate in—"

Michael Wei—Savage: "Shut up, Colmes! Nobody wants to hear what you got to say. So we're going to listen to Commie Raghead Fags now, is that what you're saying? Okay, where's it in the 10 Commandments that we should listen to Commie Raghead Fags? I don't think Thomas Jefferson or George Washington or Abraham Lincoln or any of the other Founding Fathers mentioned Communist Ragheaded Faggots. I didn't see any of those vermin mentioned in the Bill of Rights . . . ."

Molly Ivin: "In Texas we have an old saying: "You don't put syrup on a good steak. That explains how the Bush Administration can be so stupid and still conquer the world. When I'm served steak with syrup on it, I begin to get suspicious . . . ."

James Carville: "A Presidential Election is like a bunch of hound dogs down in the swamp. They all want to howl and bay and make a lot of noise. But there's always one ole hound in the pack who's willing to go right into the swamp and fetch the duck . . . ."

Mary Matalin: "My God, I'm sleeping with him!"

He rose from grim poverty and despair to conquer the town of Grimpebbet, Nebraska! He rose to the very pinnacle of power and Fame!

Now read his story.
'

BAGS TO RICHES

The new best-selling autobiography of J.D. Baghead. Learn of his birth in a public toilet, his struggles to survive, his courage in the face of enormous odds. Experience his battles with the evil neighborhood bullies.

Meet Sharon Stallmeister, his first undying love, who J.D. fondly calls, "The prostitute with the heart of gold".

Meet George Snudkey, his oldest and dearest friend. Who dies masturbating and sends a lonely John David Baghead into a downward spiral that will take him to the lowest depths of despair.

Meet Rocky Cortez, the tough but lovable street pimp Who befriends the despairing youngster and teaches him to live again, to use his talents, to rise up!

A classic story of triumph over enormous odds, BAGS TO RICHES will touch your heart, inspire you, and give you Courage!

Available in all bookstores of worth.

"Hitler, if you don't stop arguing with Stalin I'm going to bring Kiss back in here and have them perform again."
--Satan

The Great J.D. Baghead
at age 14.

NEBRASKA AGREES TO SHARE WATER WITH THIRSTY COLORADO
"When they share mountains with us," governor adds.

THE LAST WORD.....
by Pastor Milton Crane

Shakespeare was right on the money when he wrote, "Good fences make good neighbors." That advice is especially true today, when so many of our neighbors are rude and disgusting. As our community grows and changes, we must all learn to cope with the strange looking nabobs and babbling religions that threaten to overwhelm us.

Christians who were born in this fairest of prairie Communities must learn to put up "fences", physical as well as spiritual, against this tide of newcomers with their strange and frightening customs and the unpleasant odors they sometimes exude. So let us roll up our sleeves and get to work on those fences!

FROM THE UNPUBLISHED DIARY OF J. STERLING MORTON:

"My faithful servant Dudley approached me one night and said he wished to speak to me about my proposal for a national holiday urging all citizens to cut down trees...."

DR. OBESTER'S BIG JOHNSON FLEX MACHINE!

Steroid impotent? Sure they turned you into a Greek god, a hulking, masculine chick magnet. But did they also leave your most intimate features geometrically challenged? Don't be ashamed! The unfortunate reduction of certain—glands, a side effect of heavy steroid use, has caused hundreds of the world's top body builders to come to me for help.

That's why I ordered my team of medical researchers (in collaboration with scientists from NASA), to develop an effective device that would enable these poor men to regain productive and visible intimate features.

Too complicated for me to explain, you'll have to take my word for it that my BIG JOHNSON FLEX MACHINE will add millimeters to that most important intimate feature.

After you beat up her boyfriend, wouldn't you like to be able to finish the job?

"That woman works like a mule. For all that, her shape is not bad. I think I've found wife number twenty-five."
—Brigham Young

Rodney picked a fight with the young, Mild-mannered Clark Kent.

From the Unpublished Journal of Mark Twain:
"My life-long friend advised me to make some small revisions in my newest work, The Adventures of Huckleberry Finn. I listened and took his advice."

PLANNED PARENTHOOD has cancelled its scrambled eggs breakfast originally scheduled for Friday

Marshal loved—he loved—he loved—he loved his calendar girl.

"How much you want for the cow, Mrs. O"Leary?"
"What, Lucky? I could never sell her, she s my pride and joy."

PETA HEADQUARTERS CLOSED DUE TO RODENT EXTERMINATION

From the Unpublished Journal of Frank Sinatra—

"Pah-duh, pah-duh, then snap your fingers. How hard is that? But the little goombah of a saxophone player wanted to play duh-duh and not snap his fingers. He was one of those artsy-fartsy types who think the fans want interesting messages and garbage like that. He refused to do it right and reminded me that he was a union musician. The poor guy was found choked to death on his horn, a strange accident, and the tune came out pah-duh, pah-duh, snap-snap."

A pessimist gazes at clouds

From the Unpublished Journal of Lassie:
"It was one buttlick of a day. We started filming a six a.m.,
And once again that goddamned kid couldn't get it right. We
Had to shoot the scene where I rescue the little pussy from the
River eight times because he always blew his lines. Why did I
Ever let my agent talk me into going back to working with
These A-hole kids. And why don't I ever blow my lines?"

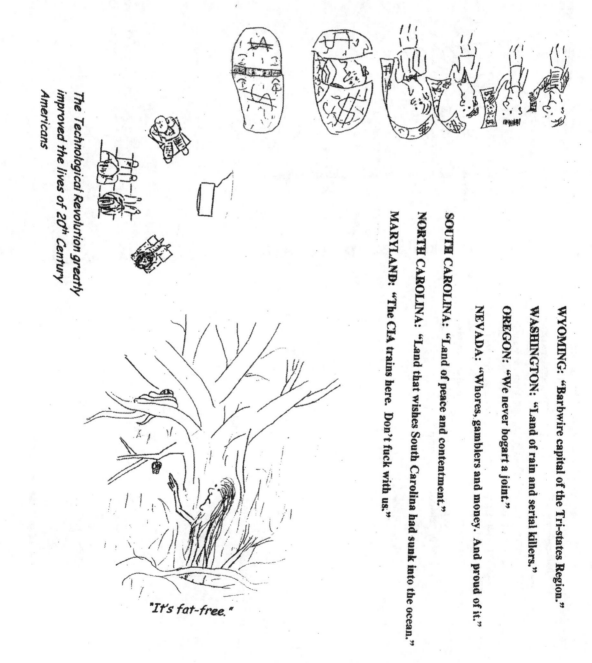

The Technological Revolution greatly improved the lives of 20th Century Americans

"It's fat-free."

WYOMING: "Barbwire capital of the Tri-states Region."

WASHINGTON: "Land of rain and serial killers."

OREGON: "We never bogart a joint."

NEVADA: "Whores, gamblers and money. And proud of it."

SOUTH CAROLINA: "Land of peace and contentment."

NORTH CAROLINA: "Land that wishes South Carolina had sunk into the ocean."

MARYLAND: "The CIA trains here. Don't fuck with us."

The Return of Cornfield Johnny:

Hey, friends, this is Cornfield Johnny! As you know, the GA caved in to my lawsuit and gave me my old editorial job back. My lawyer made theirs look like Michael Jackson's monkey, and they understood that I was not an indecent drug addict, but only a drug addict, and so they were violating my freedom of speech.

So, in defiance of the Editor, J.D. Baghead himself, and the rest of the spermless GA staff, I'm going to say a few words, and they have to let me because that's part of the settlement:

We all poop. Every animal on earth must regularly squat and perform that distasteful act known as taking a poop. Stay with me, you'll get the point of what I'm saying here. What I'm saying is, we all poop. And often with me, the poop is accompanied by great roaring farts that echo and stink far beyond the toilet.

No, don't be embarrassed, every great pope, martyr and saint at one time stank up the toilet as you and I do. With startling, explosive farts, followed by unfortunate unloading of poop.

No matter what this dishonest publication tells you, remember this, my friends: every great person in history pooped and farted on the toilet. Stink arose from the greatest of us!

Cornfield Johnny

*(The GA neither condones nor approves of Mr. Johnny's use of the word "Toilet".)

BROWN PAPER BAGS ATHLETE OF THE YEAR!

Congratulations to senior Zak McCormick, All-American Noseguard for the Unkpadema Druids.

NEBRASKA'S OWN COLLEEN AND THE YAHOO BOYS will be performing Live at the Havelock Sheep Auction And Sidewalk Sale! Hear their Latest hits, "Daddy Spanked Me Out Of Love" and "you'll Never Be Like Jesus (so we better say goodby)" Also appearing, comedian Cornfield Johnny

WHY NEBRASKA SHOULD INVADE SOUTH DAKOTA

I wrote an article for my high school newspaper about the Vietnam War, so I've had a little experience in the field of military strategy. From Alexander the Great to George Patton the basic rule has always remained the same: The best defense is a good-you know what.

The reality is, South Dakota has been planning to attack Nebraska for some time now. Dakoot cattle have been crossing over the border and grazing on Nebraska grass, armed buffalo ranchers on both sides are disputing the rich Niobrara Valley. The big shots here in Lincoln know all about it, but they won't tell you. Nor will they act until it may be too late.

Let's be blunt: we should mount an all-out offensive against South Dakota before they do it to us. To those Nebraskans among us who would rather wait and see, I have three questions: Have you learned anything from the two great world wars? Have you any pride, and are you really a true Nebraskan? And last, how much are you going to swallow from those squirrely upstarts before you catch on to their game?

They think because they have a big mountain with faces carved on it and we DON'T, that they're somehow historically and ethnically superior to us. Dakotans, they brag, are mostly Nordic, Nebraskans are mostly Slavic. That's how they see the world. They're starting to wonder if Valentine might not mind becoming a Dakoot town. And heck, as these Nebraskans are such wimp-skies, we might as well take over Lewis and Clark Lake and seize the power plant.

You have read history, and you know what ultimately happens next. Kansas aims her greedy eyes northward. Hey, the Dakoots have Nebraska on the retreat, this plays right into our hands. WE can push the Jayhawk Division up from the north and secure the key industrial city of Beatrice. Once your enemies smell blood, they will move in, and we are essentially surrounded on all sides by enemies, either real or potential.

It's true, we have a non-aggression pact with Colorado, but name one Coloradan you've ever met that you could trust. The Iowans are busy with their girlie shows and slot machines, so they will probably remain neutral. And we could count on Missouri to keep any Kansas designs in check if we were to launch a powerful offensive against the Dakoots. But we cannot hesitate, for now is the time to attack.

The truth is plain, the facts are clear. We should attack and invade their state before they do it to ours. We should move troops northeastward up the Niobrara Valley, and at the same time use the Nebraska navy to secure crossing of Lewis and Clark Lake. The surprise would be complete, and we could achieve victory over the South Dakotans in six weeks, taking the rich Black Hills for its mineral wealth. With our neighbor to the north defeated, we could then wheel our armies south and join Missouri troops for a coordinated strike at Kansas. A giant red N flag flying over the Kansas Statehouse would not be such a terrible thing.

And our borders would be secure.

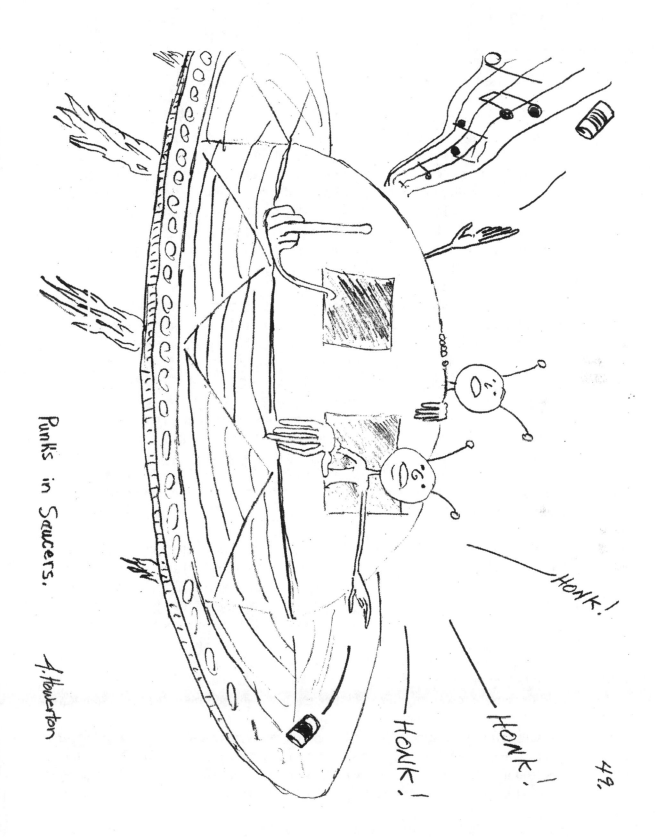

Punks in Saucers.

A. Houberton

THE LAST WORD . . . . by J.D. Baghead:

I wish we could have named this issue #2 of the Grimpebbet Almanac the Greatest GA Ever Produced. All of my staff urged me to do just that, and in so doing insinuated that we could never possibly do better, that our wads were shot into the prostitute and we could not possibly be expected to match the genius apparent in every page of GA #2. Several staff members threatened suicide, one a lawsuit, others things I cannot mention, if I, the Editor, were to even suggest beyond the nose hole of a ghost that the Almanac knows as Grimpebbet could ever produce an issue that would match our Number Two.

Posh, I coolly said to them. It can be done, and it Will be done! Our Number One was terrific. And the Number Two we did was downright epic. But the Third Issue of the Grimpebbet Almanac will be even better!

They all stared at me in horror. I was demanding of these seasoned writers that they reach deep inside themselves, that they reach down and dig out their guts and pull those guts out and splot them on the table. I was demanding nothing less than the impossible.

And you know what? Twenty-eight pounds of guts later, the impossible was created! Buy the GA #3 and you will see the impossible, Beloved Friends! It is supremely daw gon funny! We advise you, as a matter of fact, to be sitting squarely on the toilet when you read it, otherwise it is a mathematical certainty that you will piss your pants, or worse!

Exclamation points aside, don't be a fool, purchase the GA #3 and show the world you got some guts. We proved we got guts, now it's your turn. Come on, Pussies, we dare you. Buy the GA #3 if you're not chicken. Come on Puss-Puss-Pussies. If you don't buy our next issue, it's because you're scared chicken. Wah! Buy the Ga #3, Pussy Baby, if you dare. Otherwise, as we've suggested, you're a chicken's puss, and we'll slap you upside the head to prove it.

Send us money if you're not some kind of afraid punk who sniffs bicycle seats when no one is looking. When your neighbor comes up to you and says, "Hey, Sid, did you read (meaning buy), the Grimpebbet Almanac Number Three? Boy was it funny!"—how are you going to answer that neighbor and still keep any fragment of your self respect?

You're not. Not unless you've bought the GA#3 yourself and shone the world your worth. When this particularly annoying neighbor starts laughing at the stupid cartoons, you'll be able to shame him with the subtle knowledge within the GA that only Smart and Educated folks will be able to pick up.

No endeavor is more rewarding than making an ass of your neighbor. We understand this, and we want to help you. But none of this can happen if you don't purchase the GA #3.

I need to tell you this right now, though, our Beloved Friends: We have placed a curse on our third issue. I agonized over the decision to actually approve a true Voo Doo, Catholic Church, West Indian African curse, but I was convinced by my staff that only by placing a curse on our next issue could we prevent those terrible nose picking thieves out there from stealing it.

So. Pay us the five dollars we deserve, and read the GA#3 with all our blessings. You will discover wonders beyond your wildest dreams.

Read the Ga #3 and not pay for it, and the curse will unleash itself upon you. Green poisons will leak into you, goblins will sprout from your private holes and you will become a mooncalf. And that will make it apparent to your co workers and loved ones that you stole the Grimpebbet Almanac.

You all have five dollar bills, don't lie about it. Or access to a five dollar bill, one you could easily send to us. We don't want to spread virulence and curses across the land—but we will.

We promise you that the GA #3 will be worth every penny of that crappy wrinkled old five dollar bill. Husbands, do you want to see girls? Perhaps, maybe young nubile girls? A step further—young nubile girls without their clothes on? Let us complete our supposition—young nubile girls without their clothes on posed in impossibly naughty contortions?

Of course you do. Can the Grimpebbet Almanac #3 really deliver such images? Well, you'll have to be a man about it and buy the damn magazine to find out. Lori just turned 18 and she wants you. So does her best friend Amanda. But they only want you to look at them if you paid for the magazine. In other words, measly punks aren't welcome in their bedroom.

Wives, we haven't forgotten you. We have several hearty masculine staff members (myself included), who might subtly be described as "Hung like Horses". And we didn't mind exposing ourselves in the next issue at all.

But we don't want to give away the whole surprise. Buy the GA #3 for five lousy dollars, and you are forever our Beloved Friend. Don't buy it and you are rat poop, plain and simple.

The End